The
COUNTRYFINGER
STYLE**GUITAR**
Method

A Complete Guide to Travis Picking, Fingerstyle Guitar & Country Guitar Soloing

LEVI**CLAY**

FUNDAMENTAL**CHANGES**

The Country Fingerstyle Guitar Method

A Complete Guide to Travis Picking, Fingerstyle Guitar, & Country Guitar Soloing

By Levi Clay

Published by **www.fundamental-changes.com**

ISBN 978-1-911267-57-7

www.fundamental-changes.com

Twitter: **@guitar_joseph**

Over 8000 fans on Facebook: **FundamentalChangesInGuitar**

Instagram: **FundamentalChanges**

For over 250 Free Guitar Lessons with Videos Check Out

www.fundamental-changes.com

Disclaimer:

Gretsch® and Bigsby® are trademarks of Fred W. Gretsch Enterprises, Ltd., and are used herein with express written permission. All rights reserved.

Cover photos courtesy of Fred W. Gretsch Enterprises, Ltd.

Contents

Introduction

With its roots in ragtime, blues, and the pioneering Carter Family, fingerstyle and thumb-picking guitar runs deep in the veins of country music.

From Robert Johnson to Elizabeth Cotton, fingerstyle guitar has always added interest to backing parts for vocal melodies by combining the voices of bass, chords and melody.

In the '30s the style was taken to the next level and made famous by Merle Travis. Travis' use of a thumb-pick to play alternating bass patterns while picking out melodies with the index finger became so ubiquitous that nearly a century on, the style is still commonly referred to as "Travis Picking".

The late, great, Chet Atkins' deeper refinement of the technique was a natural evolution of style, and due to his huge reach as a player, producer and record executive, it became popular world over.

One anecdote you'll repeatedly hear from modern fingerpickers is that they many assumed Chet's multi-layered playing relied on recording tricks. His definition between bass and melody was so pronounced that without insider information you'd be forgiven for thinking you were hearing more than one guitar.

Chet is still considered one of the most influential and innovative guitar players the instrument has ever known; up there with the likes of Les Paul, Jimi Hendrix, and Charlie Christian.

The next big name associated with the style is "The Alabama Wild Man", Jerry Reed. Reed's style was born from the lineage of Merle and Chet, but delivered with ground-breaking flair and innovation.

Chet, Merle, and Reed are the three names considered the "unspoken influences". They're the pillars of the style and you should know their work inside out.

However, the list of pioneers doesn't end there. With trailblazers like Buster B Jones, Tommy Emmanuel, Thom Bresh, Scotty Anderson, Doyle Dykes, Richard Smith, Brooks Robertson, and Martin Tallstrom (just to name a few), finger-picking is still very much alive and well.

Get the Audio

The audio files for this book are available to download for free from **www.fundamental-changes.com** and the link is in the top right corner. Simply select this book title from the drop-down menu and follow the instructions to get the audio.

We recommend that you download the files directly to your computer, not to your tablet, and extract them there before adding them to your media library. You can then put them on your tablet, iPod or burn them to CD.

On the download page there is a help PDF and we also provide technical support via the contact form.

Kindle / eReaders

To get the most out of this book, remember that you can double tap any image to enlarge it. Turn off 'column viewing' and hold your kindle in landscape mode.

For over 250 Free Guitar Lessons with Videos Check out:

www.fundamental-changes.com

Twitter: **@guitar_joseph**

FB: **FundamentalChangesInGuitar**

Instagram: **FundamentalChanges**

Get the Tone – Guitars and Amps

When it comes to country fingerstyle, there are a surprisingly wide variety of guitar tones created by the great players and the sound you want will be influenced by the players you enjoy.

The most iconic country guitars are, without a doubt, the Gretsch hollow-bodies made famous by Chet Atkins. Be it the 6120, or the Country Gentleman, these guitars have a unique sound due to the Bigsby tremolo system and highly sensitive Filter'Tron pickups. They're not essential to the style but are responsible for a big part of Chet's iconic tone.

Merle Travis, the father of the style, played a selection of guitars and even had solid body electrics made for him before Leo Fender launched the Broadcaster. For the most part, Merle switched between various high-end acoustic guitars and semi-hollows like the Gibson 400.

Jerry Reed found his voice on the classical-style guitar and preferred the tone of nylon strings. His most iconic guitar was a modified 1968 Baldwin electric-classical with extreme cutaway. While he was occasionally seen with a Telecaster, the nylon-string was his trademark.

When Jerry's popularity grew, many companies made a move on the portable nylon string market, although few matched the quality of the Godin Multiac guitars. These were favoured by players like Buster B Jones and now Doyle Dykes. They combine the tone and feel of a nylon string with the portability and ease-of-amplification of an electric guitar.

Then there are the more traditional steel-string acoustics favoured by the likes of Tommy Emmanuel (who has a signature Maton guitar) and Marcel Dadi (who was often seen sporting an Ovation).

My personal choices (and the ones you'll hear on the accompanying for the recordings) are the Godin Multiac, Sigma steel string, Gibson Howard Roberts, and Fender Telecaster. I lean towards the sound and feel of nylon strings myself, but appreciate the range of the tonal options found in many different instruments.

When it comes to amplification, something clean is the obvious choice. Chet used a 25-watt Standel made in 1954 on countless recordings, and occasionally a selection of more powerful amps like a Paul Rivera-modified Fender Princeton and the MusicMan RD-50s.

Many of the greats would just use a direct inject (DI) box straight to the PA system; it's all about hearing the guitar in its purest form.

My recording setup is direct into my computer via an RME Babyface Pro with effects provided by various Toontrack plugins. Things have certainly come a long way from the high-quality ribbon mics of Chet's day (though that's still a great option if you have thousands of dollars to spend!).

Don't worry about the instrument for now. Turn your mind towards technique, chords and vocabulary. By the end of this book you'll have a better idea of what sound you want to create.

Part One: Technique Primer

In this section, you will learn the basics of Country Fingerstyle Guitar. While this style wasn't born out of academia, take comfort in the knowledge that approaching the genre so methodically will result in accelerated results.

This section covers:

- Introduction to the thumb pick

- Finger-picking skills

- Basic chords

- Alternating bass notes

- The "pinch" techniqueSyncopated melodies

- Melodic articulation

- Advanced chords

The skills covered here will prepare you to tackle any Travis-picked classic. While it's possible to skip over any of these sections, each has been carefully written to strengthen the fundamental building blocks of the style. Giving each concept the time and respect it deserves will ultimately lead to fewer challenges when tackling the more complicated ideas later.

The fundamental lesson here is one of rhythm. While you will cover many chords and melodic patterns, learning the following precise rhythms and syncopated melodies will make the more advanced ideas in Part Two much easier. Even the simplest exercise should be practiced with a metronome until you achieve an almost zen-like state; completely automatic playing that locks into the click.

The styles covered in this book are often used by singers, so once you feel your guitar part lock into the pulse, try singing a melody. It's not about sounding good; it's about ensuring the pulse is so ingrained in your thumb and fingers that the playing can be done unconsciously while focusing on another task. Practice singing and playing; I promise you'll thank me later!

Chapter One: Thumb Picks & Alternating Bass

There's no avoiding the fact that almost every great country fingerstyle player used a thumb pick. While it's possible to play most country vocabulary with the bare thumb or with pick and fingers (hybrid picking), the thumb pick creates strong tone and definition for the bass notes. It also allows you to keep all your fingers free for playing chords and melodies.

Playing with a thumb pick may feel awkward at first. A good thumb pick will be tight enough that it's unable to move or slip off, although it's possible that the pick squeezing on your thumb can cut off its circulation. If this is the case, putting the pick in hot water will soften the material and allow it to adjust to the shape of your thumb.

There are many thumb picks on the market and different players prefer different styles, although classic Dunlop picks are a common choice. I use the D'Addario model as the tip is a little rounder and I'm extremely fond of the Jim Kelly Bumblebee which features a Jazz III style pick attached to the thumb grip. This can be angled from side to side and pushed back and forward to get the perfect amount of pick on the strings.

The best way to get to grips with a thumb pick is to play some of the basic alternating bass patterns that are a staple of country guitar.

First up, here are some examples using chords with a 5th-string root. The chord diagrams for these chords are shown below.

Example 1a:

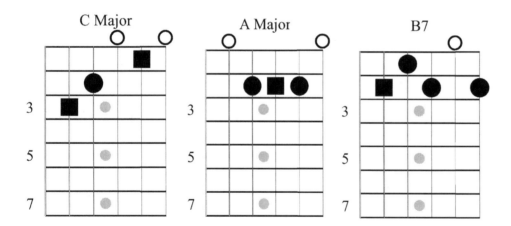

When playing chords that have root notes on the 5th string, it's normal to use a bass-note pattern that plays the 5th string, the 4th string, the 6th string, and finally the 4th string again.

Play the following example on an open C major chord. The *intervals* of the chord played in the bass are the root, 3rd, 5th and then the root again.

Example 1b:

When you listen to the recording, you may notice I apply some *palm muting*. Palm muting isn't always used, but it certainly helps to add some definition between the bass notes and melodies you'll add later. In order to palm mute, place the fleshy side of the palm (on the side of your little finger) on the strings by the bridge.

Even though you only play one note at a time, the full chord is held throughout. The reason for this will become clear when we add a finger-picked melody later.

The next example applies the same picking pattern to an open A major chord. You may notice that you play different intervals of the chord even though you are using the same picking pattern. In this example you play the root, 5th, 5th and then the root again. Bass patterns don't need to be uniform; they're all about playing a consistent rhythm to drive the music forward to create a bed for the melody to sit on.

Example 1c:

Next, apply the same picking pattern to a B7 chord.

Example 1d:

Here are three chord voicings with the roots on the low E string.

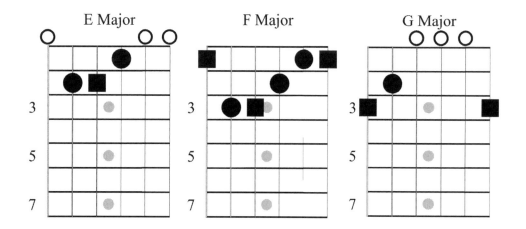

Chord voicings with the root on the low E string, require a new picking pattern. The two common patterns are:

6th, 4th, 5th, 4th, and

6th, 4th, 6th, 4th.

Here's the first pattern on an open E chord.

Example 1e:

Here's the same pattern on an open G major chord.

Example 1f:

It's common to alternate exclusively between the 6th and 4th strings. Here's it is demonstrated on the G major chord. Remember to hold the full chord down throughout the exercise.

Example 1g:

It's possible to use both patterns. The purpose of the thumb is to imply harmony and create a driving rhythm, not necessarily to create a consistent melody.

In the next example I apply both picking patterns to a barred F major chord.

Example 1h:

It's also possible (though less common) to use chords with the root on the D string. When this happens it's usual to pick the 4th, 3rd, 5th, and 3rd strings.

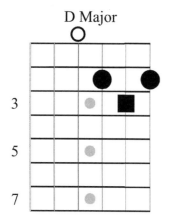

Example 1i:

Voicings like this are often avoided as they restrict melodic options and create a bass line that's a little too high pitched to be defined against the melody.

Now to apply the previous picking patterns to some country chord progressions.

First up is a chord progression found in the Merle Travis classic, Nine Pound Hammer and consists of nothing more than E major, A major, and B7. The secret here is not to confuse the picking patterns for each chord. If you need to, refer to the previous exercises and take more time to cover the material accurately.

Example 1j:

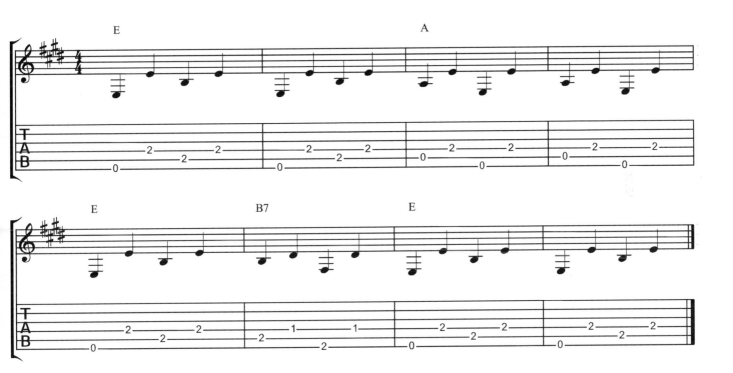

Here's a longer example that works to the traditional Elizabeth Cotton tune, Freight Train.

Cotton was left handed but played a right-handed guitar flipped over, and so played the alternating bass parts with her the finger while the melody was played by the thumb. It's well worth seeking out some videos of her on YouTube.

Example 1k:

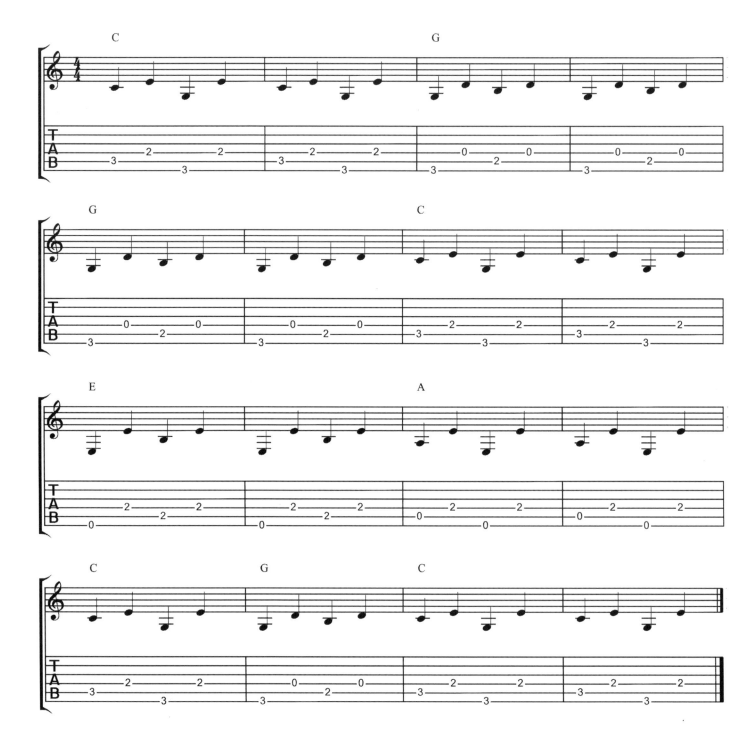

Here's one inspired by the 1915 song, Are You From Dixie? This song became a hit for Jerry Reed over 40 years later in 1969. As this one is longer, it may help to learn the vocal melody to the song to familiarize yourself with where the chords change.

Example 1l:

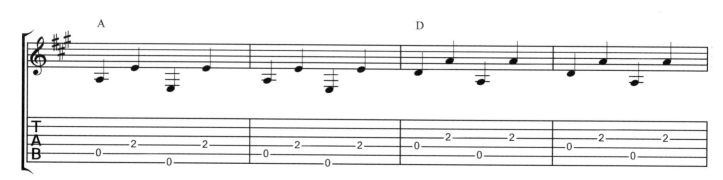

Chapter Two: The Pinch Technique

It's nearly time to add melodies to your alternating bass patterns, but let's first explore some notation conventions to help you quickly develop your musicianship and understand how country music is written.

The following example shows some more advanced Travis picking vocabulary. Without learning it, take a look at the rhythmic notation.

Example 2a:

While it can be read, it certainly doesn't make your life easy or present the music in the spirit with which it's played. Travis picking is about the interplay between two separate voices; the bass part played with the thumb, and the melody played with the fingers.

This next example makes the thumb and melody parts much clearer to see. The thumb strokes are notated with downward stems and the melody is notated with upward stems. It's a small difference, but as you begin to develop your technique you'll find that viewing the notation as two individual parts will help you learn it much more quickly.

Example 2b:

Each exercise in this book is notated using this convention to allow you to break down something that sounds complicated into individual parts that work together.

The Pinch

The first technique used to pick melodies is often referred to as the *pinch* because it's played with a pinching motion when the bass note and melody note are played simultaneously.

Here's an example of that technique played on an open C major chord. I've not included any alternating bass part here; simply a low C bass note played with the thumb, and a high C plucked with the index finger. Hold down the full C Major chord throughout.

Example 2c:

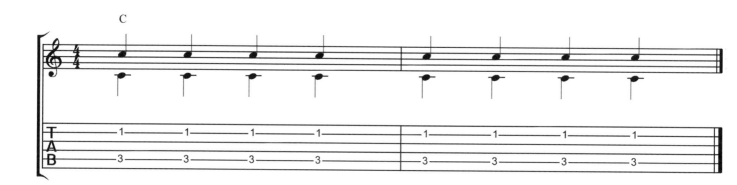

While the players who followed him would use multiple fingers to play melodies, Merle Travis only ever used his index finger.

The following example is similar to the one above, but now the index finger moves to the adjacent string to play a different note.

Example 2d:

The next example takes this approach further with the index finger moving between three strings.

Example 2e:

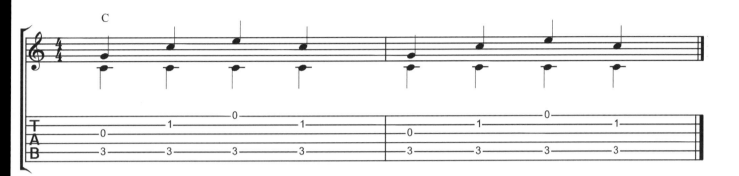

Now you have this basic pinch idea under your fingers, study the following example. It features an alternating bass pattern with a melody that is pinched and held throughout the bar.

Apply a light palm mute to the bass while allowing the melody to ring freely over the top.

Example 2f:

While the pinch technique is simple in execution, it doesn't mean you have to limit the rhythms played in the melody line.

The next example combines the open C alternating bass pattern with a melody that begins on beat 2. The chord is held while the thumb plays the first bass note before the melody note is pinched on beat 2. Beats 3 and 4 continue the alternating bass pattern while the melody note rings through.

A clear palm mute on the bass notes will help separate the bass and melody parts for the listener and create the illusion of two instruments playing together.

Example 2g:

Here's another exercise that features an alternating bass pattern and a simple descending and ascending scale.

The aim of any exercise like this is to make the bass line automatic and unconscious. Don't think of the bass and melody as two separate lines (despite it being exactly that), the thumb should be automatic while your attention is focused on melody.

Example 2h:

This next example takes the basic idea from the previous exercise and applies it to a G major chord.

Example 2i:

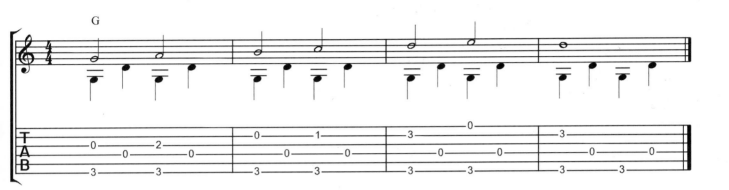

Here's a version of a chord sequence you've seen before. As with the last two examples, the pinch is played on beats 1 and 3.

Example 2j:

The next example was inspired by The Animals' classic, House of the Rising Sun, and in this stripped-back form it also conjures up images of The Beatles.

It introduces a new chord in bar 3, a D/F#. This is simply the D major chord you already know with the 3rd (F#) played in the bass. While this is primarily played to create a smooth descending bass line (A – G – F# - F) it has the added benefit of containing a low note on the E string that gives a little more range than a normal 4th string root.

Example 2k:

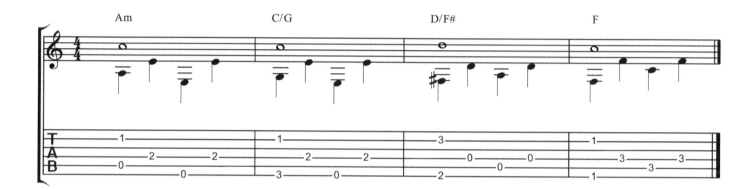

It is possible to create interesting melodic ideas with pinches on beats other than 1 or 3. Here's another simple melody on a basic chord progression.

Example 2l:

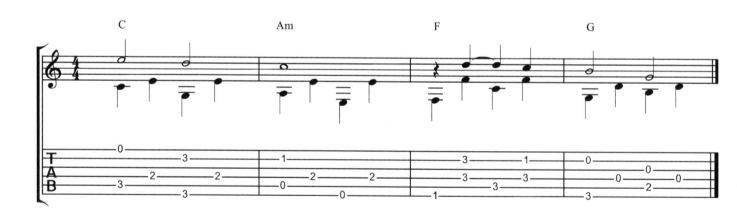

The next example is a stripped back version of Nine Pound Hammer from the previous chapter. It may present a challenge with the consecutive pinches in the second bar, but technique-wise it's nothing new. Take it slowly, and make sure the thumb-picked bass part is completely programmed.

Example 2m:

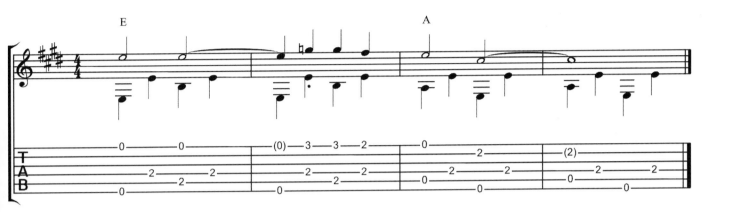

Finally, here's the American folk song, Camptown Races in the key of G using the pinch technique to play the melody against the chord accompaniment.

Example 2n:

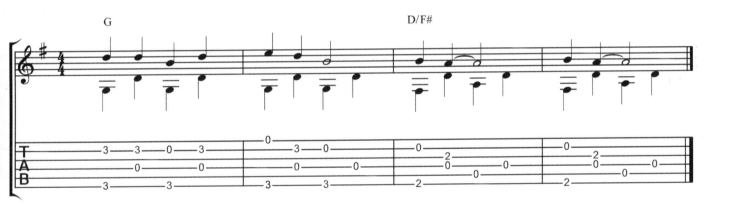

Simple melodies like this form the early foundations of compelling Travis picking and the pinch is fundamental to the country style Practice until you're able to lock into the pulse because it won't be easy to add even basic syncopation if you're not confident playing melodies on the beat first.

Chapter Three: Introducing Syncopation

Syncopation is the use of a rhythm that is in some way unexpected and places the melody notes *off the beat*. All examples up to this point have been unsyncopated and have consisted of notes played *on the beat*.

Adding syncopation to a melody really brings country fingerpicking to life and helps to create the impression of two individual instruments playing together.

The first example introduces a syncopated pickup note leading into the first bar. When counting out loud "one and two and three and four and", the first note is played on the 'and' of beat 4.

The melody note rings throughout the bar before being played again on the 'and' of beat 4 and held throughout the next bar.

Example 3a:

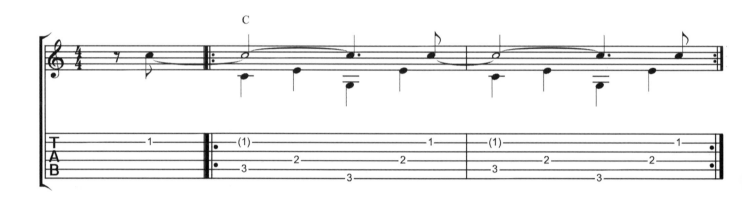

This technique results in a feeling of alternation between the thumb and first finger, which should help you to keep time.

The next example is similar but moves the syncopated melody note to the 'and' of beat 1.

Example 3b:

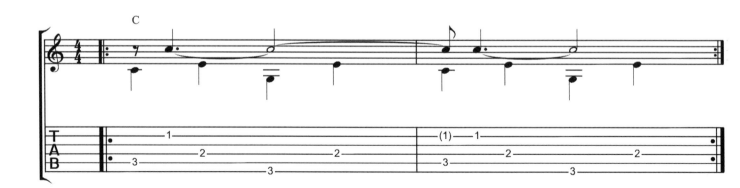

Now the syncopated note is moved to the 'and' of 2 and applied to an E chord. To keep things interesting the melodic note alternates between the G string and the B string.

Example 3c:

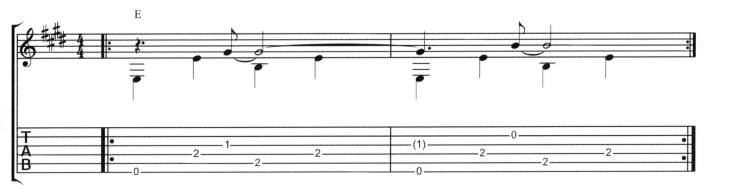

Finally, the syncopation is moved to the 'and' of 3.

Example 3d:

It's possible to add syncopation to multiple notes in a bar. Here's an example in G with a syncopated note played on the 'and' of beats 2 and 3.

Example 3e:

Here's an example where a syncopated note has been added to every beat. When playing busier examples like this, it's important to use palm muting to create definition between the bass notes and the sustained melody. To help you to hear this, I've recorded it correctly first, then let everything ring out on the second time through.

Example 3f:

Syncopation comes to life when you start combining pinched and syncopated notes. Here's a common played on a C major chord which features a pinch on beat 2 and syncopation on the 'and' of 3.

Example 3g:

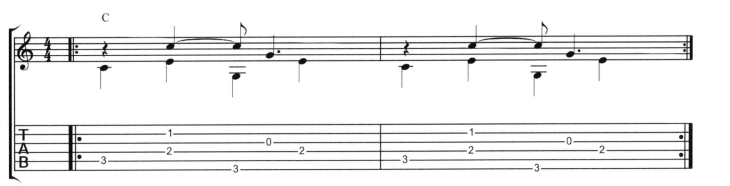

Here's the same rhythmic idea applied to a chord progression. There's no real melody being played here, you're just plucking a note from the chord to create some rhythmic interest. This would be a good rhythmic "bed" to sing over if you were a solo performer.

Example 3h:

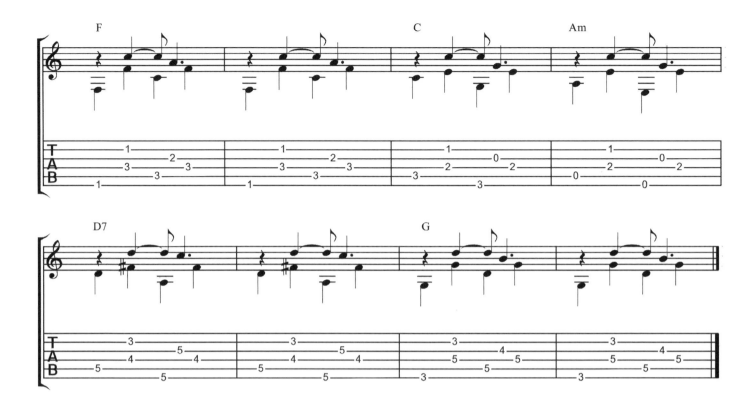

Using syncopation, it's possible to play simple melodies against chord changes to make fuller sounding songs.

This example uses a pinch on beat 1 with syncopation on the 'and' of 2 to create a more intricate version of Freight Train.

Example 3i:

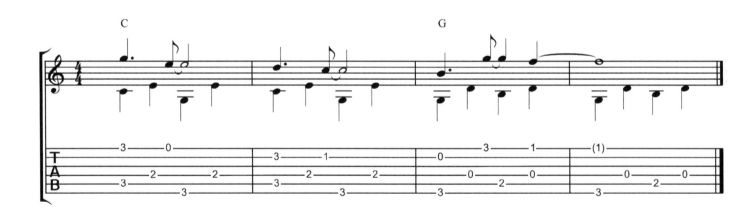

Too much repetition or predictability can quickly bore a listener, so mixing various pinches and syncopations is a good way to keep your audience guessing and develop your technical capabilities.

This example is based on the previous idea but adds variation in alternating bars to keep it interesting. Try using this picking pattern with example 3h.

Example 3j:

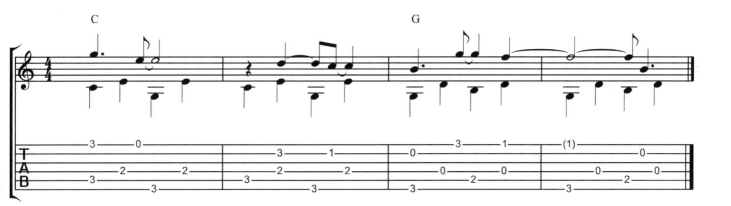

Here's another example based on House of the Rising Sun that mixes different combinations of pinches and syncopations.

Patterns like this are normally improvised. At this stage that may seem impossible, but as you develop your technique you'll naturally start to use the index finger to create interesting rhythms over an "automatic" bass line.

Example 3k:

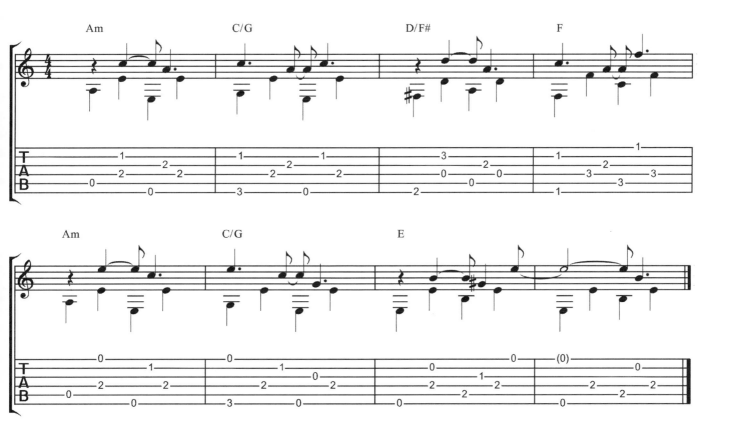

Finally, here's a syncopated arrangement that draws influence from Nine Pound Hammer. Compare it to example 2m to see just how much interest the syncopation adds.

Example 3l:

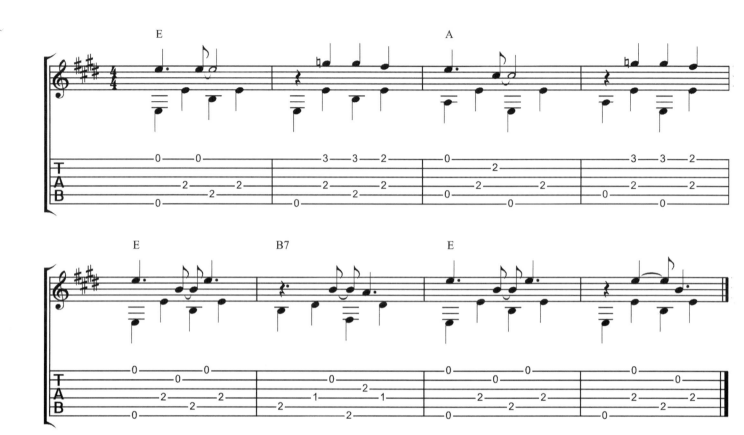

There are still some techniques that you'll need to master to play this style, but focus on getting to grips with pinches and syncopation before moving on. If can play the chords shapes, using the index finger to pick out a melody shouldn't pose a challenge.

Chapter Four: Melodic Articulation

When playing a melody, there are two things to consider; *which* notes you're going to play, and *how* you're going to play them. There are many ways to play a note: you could play it quietly, you could slide into it, you could bend up to the note, etc. This aspect of playing is called *articulation* and refers to *how you play and transition between notes*.

We've already looked at one form of articulation with the palm mute technique but there are many more ways to articulate notes.

Another form of articulation to consider is *staccato*. Staccato literally means "detached", and can be interpreted as playing notes with short, detached rhythms A staccato note is indicated by a dot above or below the note head. The note is played, and then quickly muted by either lightly lifting the fretting hand finger or by stopping the string with the picking hand.

The following example is first played with the melody ringing out, and then played with a staccato articulation. Listen carefully to the audio recording to pick up on the differences in sound.

Example 4a:

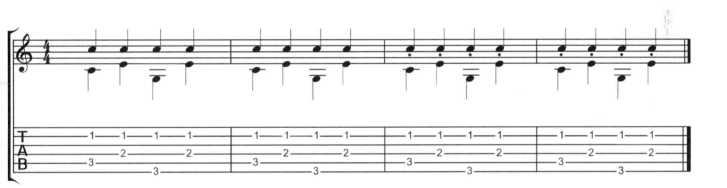

Here's that staccato concept applied to a melodic idea. The staccato note adds dynamic interest and a degree of playfulness.

Example 4b:

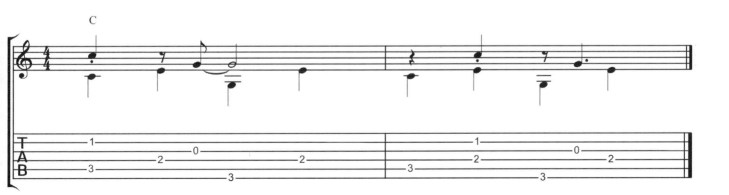

While staccato does create a different sound, hammer-ons and pull-offs are more dramatic because they allow you to use the fretting hand to add more notes to a melody without having to overwork the picking hand fingers.

The following C major example begins with a pinch on beat 1 which is hammered on to the 1st fret of the B string.

Example 4c:

This same idea could be articulated with a *grace note*. This means that the hammer isn't given full rhythmic value. So rather than playing the open B and hammering to the C note an 1/8th note later, the B is played and *instantly* hammered to C. This small difference makes a big change to the sound of the melody.

Example 4d:

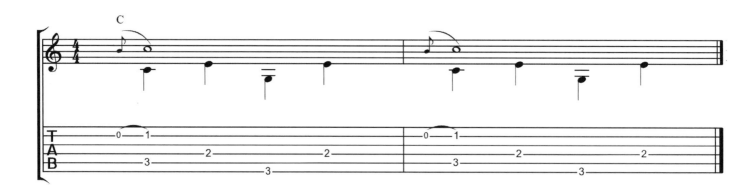

Hammer-ons from an open string allow you to create intricate melodies, as the example below shows.

Example 4e:

Here's an example that isolates that hammer-on technique on the C major chord.

Example 4f:

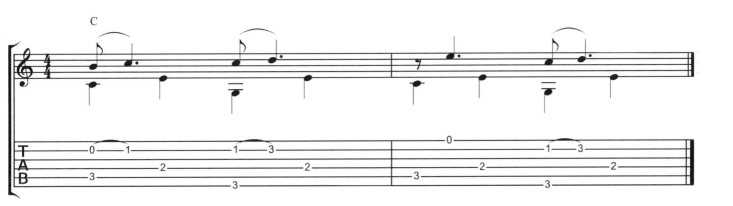

This next example uses a hammer-on to play the melody in the B section of Freight Train. Use the first finger to barre and play the F on the high E string.

Example 4g:

So far, we have applied hammer-ons to the pinch, but we can also apply this technique to syncopated notes too. It can be a challenge to keep a hammered note the same volume as a plucked note so it doesn't get drowned out by the bass.

Here's that basic mechanic applied to an open E major chord. Take it slow, and try to play the hammer-ons with an equal volume to the picked notes.

Example 4h:

Here's a trickier example that uses the same rhythm but moves to a 1st inversion chord (E7/G#) in bar two. Allowing these melodies to ring out is tricky; the new chord should be held while the note you're hammering from is plucked.

Example 4i:

Here's an example with a syncopated hammer-on played later in the bar.

Example 4j:

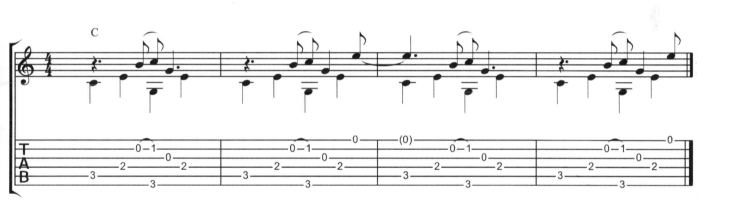

Next up is a more complicated example that moves between C major and A minor. The melody features both syncopated hammer-ons and a pinched pull-off in the final bar.

Example 4k:

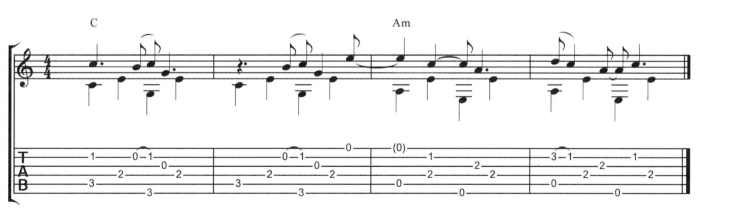

It's also possible to use these techniques in the thumb part. The alternating bass pattern is played as expected but the open D string is hammered on to the E note.

Example 4l:

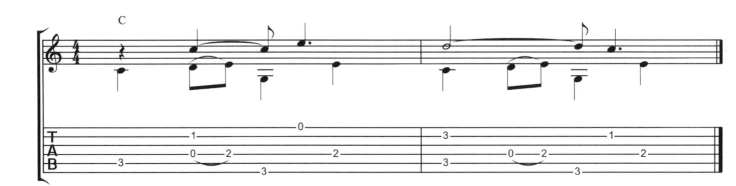

When melodies are added to the bass, we can create some very interesting musical ideas. Travis was a master of this sort of thing and would often play intricate bass lines for entire sections of songs.

This next example uses hammer-ons and pull-offs in the melody and bass to move from one chord to the next every four bars.

Example 4m:

There are many more applications of these techniques and we will look at them later as your technique becomes more internalised.

Chapter Five: Advanced Chord Positions

Not all chords played in country are played in the open position of the neck. While there's nothing inherently wrong with open chords (and you'll find that most playing is done in this area), sometimes there's great benefit to be had by visiting the dusty end of the neck.

Aside from more voicing options, the obvious reason to move up the neck is to access higher melody notes in the melody. In the open position, the highest note you can comfortably reach is probably the G# on the 4th fret of the E string.

This can be problematic if you play a Travis picked classic like Mr Sandman where you need to play a C# at the 9th fret as one of the melody notes. Chet Atkins even plays the 12th fret on the B string for one section.

With a basic knowledge of triad inversions and the CAGED system, it is relatively easy to shift up and down the neck.

The following chord diagrams show an A major chord played in three different areas of the neck. The first is in the open position (based around an open A major chord), The second is played at the 5th fret (based around an open E major chord shape), and the third has a root at the 12th fret (based around an open C major chord shape).

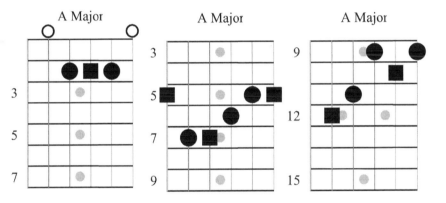

In each of these positions, it's possible to play the notes on the highest 4 strings against the open A string, as you're always going play a fragment of an A major chord.

Example 5a:

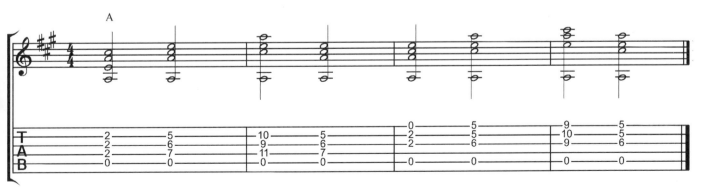

If you play the top four notes of each shape and add an alternating bass pattern of 5th string, 4th string, 6th string, 4th string, you can access three areas of the neck and cover twelve frets easily.

This example demonstrates those patterns. The chord shapes you should hold down are shown with brackets.

Example 5b:

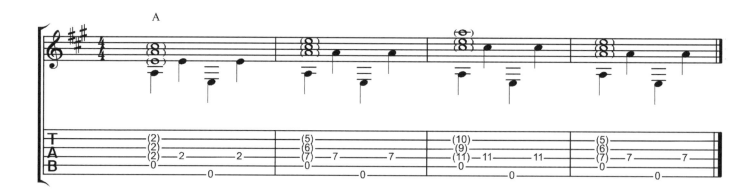

Here are those same three positions played with a simple melodic idea from the previous chapter. The picking hand mechanic is the same as before, the only thing that's changed is the fretting hand location.

Example 5c:

It's possible to add notes on the higher strings to make melodies, as this example around the E shape shows.

Example 5d:

Here's a melody higher up on the neck in the C shape. It's the same idea in a new chord shape.

Example 5e:

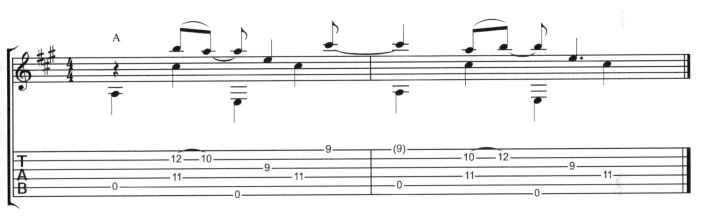

The next example shifts between the E and C shapes so that the melody can freely move to wherever feels right. While the bass part does change slightly, the ear simply hears the implied A major chord and focuses on the melodic detail.

Example 5f:

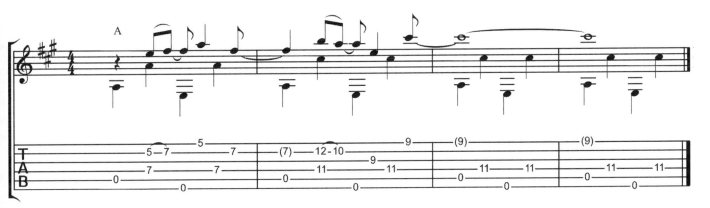

These ideas can also be applied to an E major chord too. The following example is the melody from Example 5b but now in E major.

For consistency, the thumb alternates between the 6th and 4th strings only.

Example 5g:

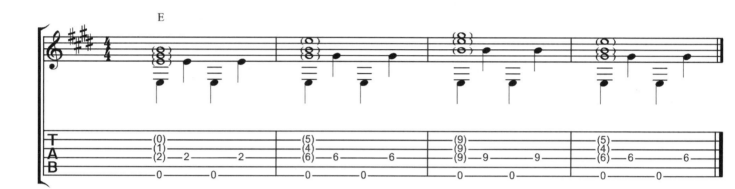

It's possible to shift up through the whole neck via each pattern.

Example 5h:

Here's a melodic idea around an E major chord in the C shape.

Example 5i:

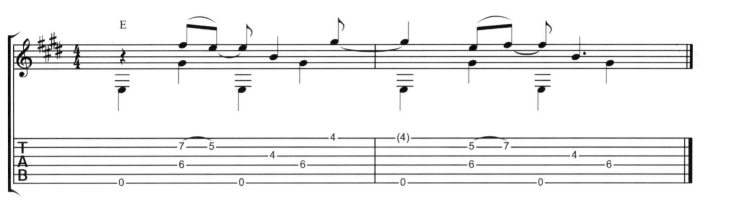

This next example reaches all the way up to the 12th fret. Ideas like this were often heard in the playing of rockabilly players like Scotty Moore.

Example 5j:

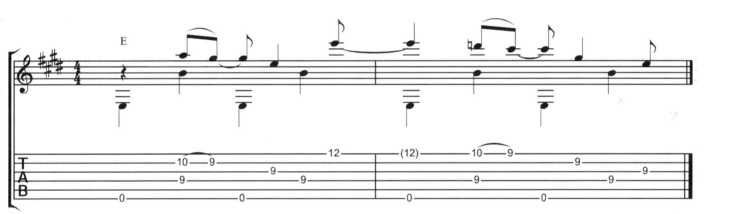

Now combine some of these positions to outline an E major chord. Familiarise yourself with the bass line before adding the melody. It's all about learning how the melody interacts with the bass, don't just try to play both lines and hope it all works out OK!

Example 5k:

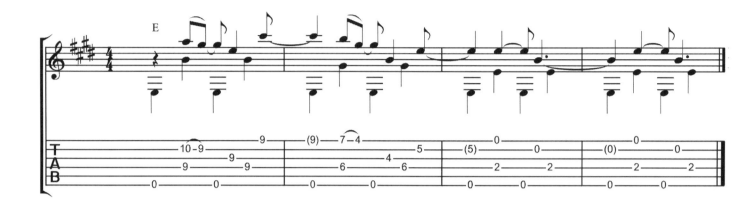

This final example draws influence from the Merle Travis classic, Cannonball Rag. The basic idea is a series of dominant 7 chords moving around *the circle of 5ths*. To keep things interesting, I've used some more advanced, higher-position voicings for the E and A chords then used basic barre forms for the D and G chords in the same area of the neck.

Example 5l:

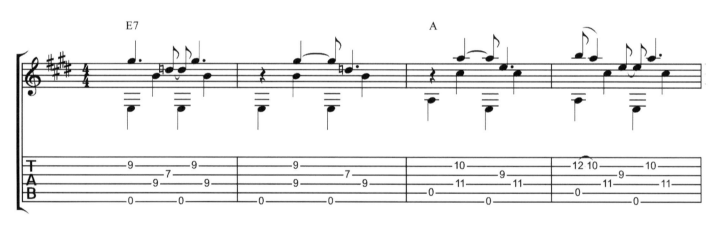

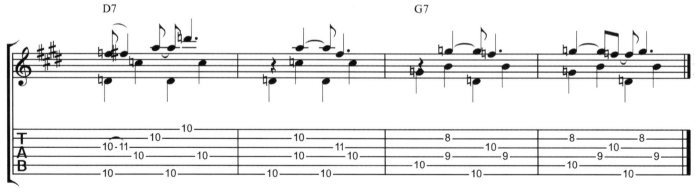

There are enough techniques presented in these first five chapters to keep you busy for a while. Take your time with each concept as it's important to have a solid understanding of the techniques used before moving on to Part Two where you'll learn the idiosyncrasies and evolution of fingerstyle by studying Merle Travis, Chet Atkins, and Jerry Reed.

Before progressing, the thumb should be automatic when playing alternating bass patterns. The fingers should be comfortable playing melodies both on the beat (the pinch technique), and with syncopation.

You mind should not be occupied by the bass line so are free to think about the tone of each note you play. If you feel like you're on the edge of your ability when playing the bass and melody parts together, don't be afraid to spend more time on the rudiments before moving on.

There's no rush: the strongest houses are built on the most solid of foundations.

Part Two: Masters of the Style

In this section, you'll be taught the stylistic idiosyncrasies of three key players in the history of country fingerstyle guitar: Merle Travis, Chet Atkins and Jerry Reed. While they aren't the only important country fingerstyle players, each can be considered a step in the evolution of Travis picking.

By studying each player individually you'll develop a deep understanding how the techniques covered so far can help you to develop dramatically different sounds.

In the previous section you developed the basic picking hand technique of playing an alternating bass line with the thumb and a melody with the fingers. In Part Two, the goal is to focus on how your music *sound*s, not just how it is played. There's a big difference between the very deliberate, articulate playing of Chet Atkins, and the more rough and ready approach you hear in the playing of Merle Travis.

Pay careful attention to the recorded examples (both in the book, and the original artists), as getting the tone right is the one of the most important aspects of playing the guitar. There's a big difference between music on the page and music that will touch people for generations. It's all about the sound, so don't be afraid to spend time making the examples sound great, not just "correct".

Chapter Six: Merle Travis Style

While perhaps not the originator of the style, there's no denying that Merle Travis put a face to the sound of Travis picking. The sad truth is that the early record industry was particularly exploitative to artists. So while musicians like Elizabeth Cotton became well known in her later life, in the 1930s her name was unknown to many music fans.

In the blues and ragtime tradition, there are plenty of artists whose music you may have heard but not been able to name. One example would be Blind Blake; a man of whom very little is known. Record companies knew enough to put a microphone in front of him and make records, but it's still hotly debated as to his cause of death, location of birth, or even his real name. This is a tragedy as Blake was a talented musician who had an impressive mastery of playing ragtime piano on the guitar.

The "Travis Technique" is not something Merle Travis invented, but definitely something he popularized. In fact, Freight Train was composed before Merle was even born, so who knows what amazing talents we missed before the advent of audio recording.

Born in 1917, Merle Travis developed the fingerpicking technique commonly used in his home state of Kentucky. This style was passed down from person to person, with notable names including Arnold Shultz (a travelling coalman), and Kennedy Jones (the original composer of Cannonball Rag).

Merle Travis' picking style used almost exclusively the thumb and index finger alone. In that respect, Part One of this book should have you well prepared. The area where Merle's playing shows some variance is in the strokes executed by the thumb.

As a quick reminder, the country alternating bass pattern looks something like this:

Example 6a:

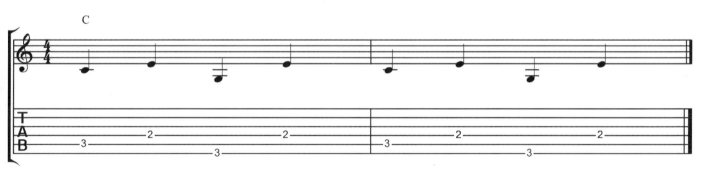

Merle's strokes were usually considerably broader and created a richer sound when playing accompaniment.

The concept of playing "low, high, low, high" is still present, but now instead of playing single notes the thumb is less precise and plays a few strings at once.

Example 6b:

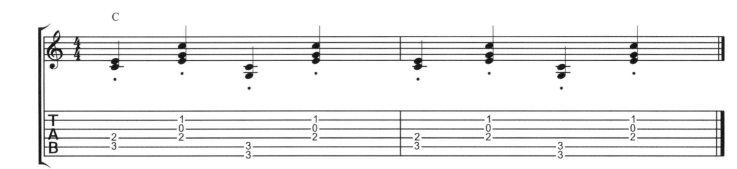

Remember that this is not a precise art. just think about striking the guitar low then high and letting whatever is hit ring out. When holding a chord, any selection of the notes I hit should sound ok. It wasn't uncommon for Merle to hit *all* the higher strings on beats 2 and 4 if that's what the melody required.

Merle's style used a wide variety of barre chords. Here's an alternating bass pattern applied to G chord at the third fret. While it's described as a barre chord, Merle fretted the note on the low E string with his thumb, and used the fingers to fret the notes on the A, D, G, and B strings.

Example 6c:

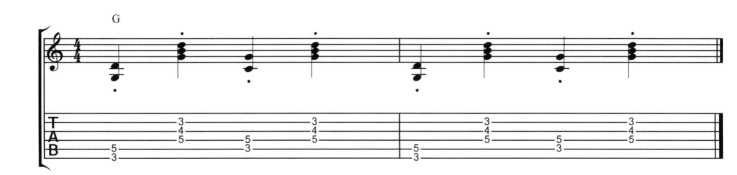

This example uses the same broad strokes but now with a D9 barre chord; another voicing often played by Merle.

Example 6d:

Here's an example drawn from the Isham Jones standard, I'll See You in My Dreams. This is a classic of the genre with both Merle, and later Chet Atkins (with Mark Knopfler) recording versions. It uses chord voicings from the previous three examples transposed to a different key.

Example 6e:

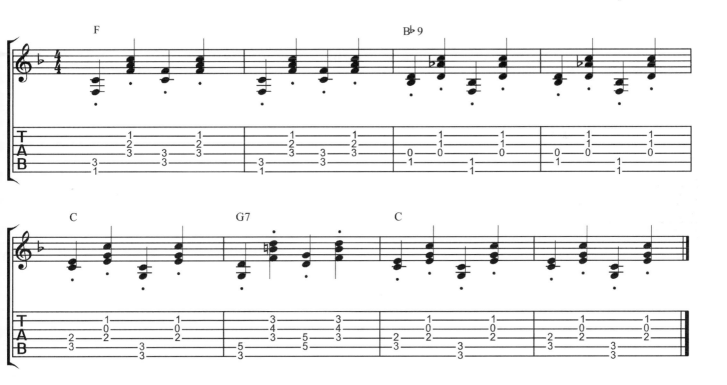

The following example draws from Merle's comedy classic, Smoke! Smoke! Smoke! You'll notice an A barre chord form that was used in Example 6c, but rather than playing the A string on beat 3, the thumb is lifted to play an open E.

You'll also notice that the final bar contains a melodic pattern in the bass to walk from the final A chord back to the first A chord on the repeat.

Example 6f:

This example draws on the chord progression from Fat Gal and again uses chord voicings covered earlier.

Example 6g:

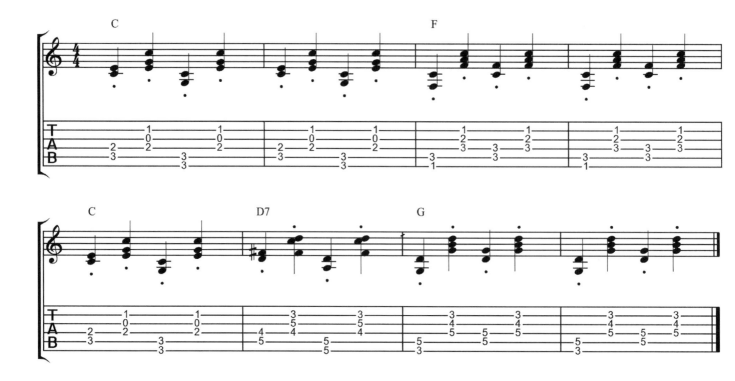

For the sake of comparison, here's the same example played with more deliberate picking-hand articulation. It doesn't sound bad, but it certainly doesn't sound like Merle Travis.

Example 6h:

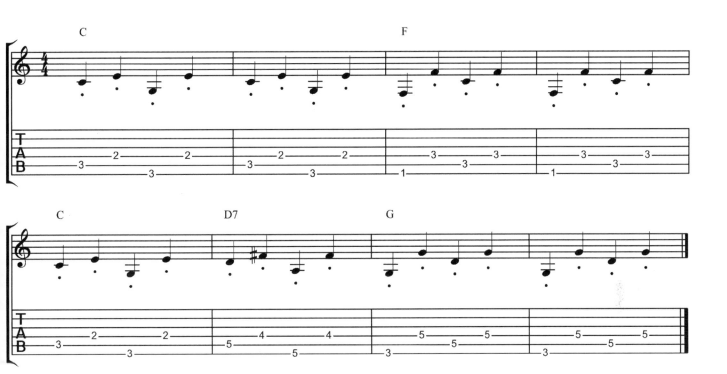

Now to add the index finger!

This example includes a syncopated note on the 'and' of beat 3. There's nothing new on the melody front, but playing this syncopation against the broader Merle-style thumb strokes may be difficult at first.

Example 6i:

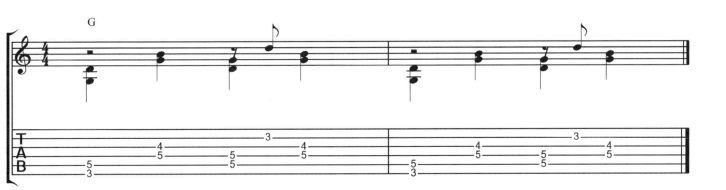

This next example is a common Merle pattern played on songs like Nine Pound Hammer. The most challenging aspect is the two consecutive notes played with the index finger on beat 3. This is made easier by the swing feel as it gives you a little more time to play the second note.

Example 6j:

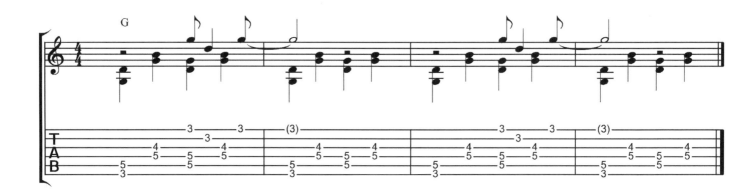

Now let's apply the same concept to a D9 chord and add two more syncopated notes in bar two. The first time these are played on a static note, but on the repeat they walk up chromatically to the note B. This variation may feel difficult at first but does occur regularly in country songs like Cannonball Rag, so practice here will pay off later.

Example 6k:

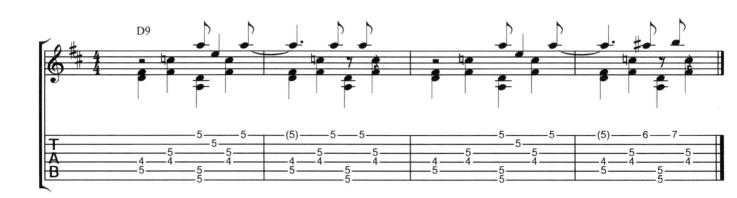

The previous two ideas are used here to outline the G major and C9 chords in Nine Pound Hammer.

Example 6l:

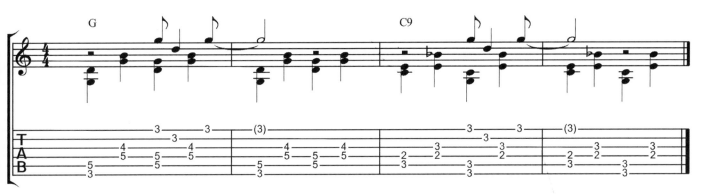

Here's the same idea but now with a bass part that walks up from G to C at the end of the second bar.

Example 6m:

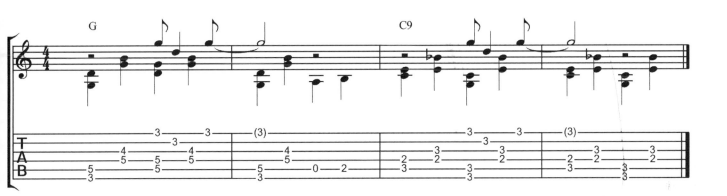

The next example is similar but adds a D7 chord in the second half of bars two and four. This creates harmonic interest without moving away from the original chord progression.

Example 6n:

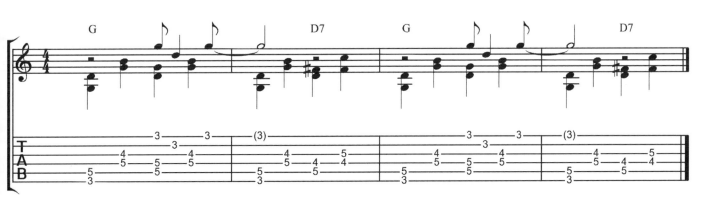

Here's a C7 variation you can play instead of the C9 chord in example 6m. If Merle wanted to play a regular C7 chord he might have opted for one like this.

This is quite tricky as the thumb needs to play both the E and A string.

Example 6o:

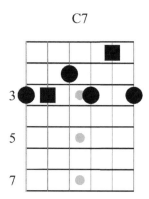

Here's that chord voicing used with the melody from the last few examples. When playing this chord, Merle would often aim for a 6, 4, 6, 4 picking pattern (with his wide strikes hitting more strings).

Example 6p:

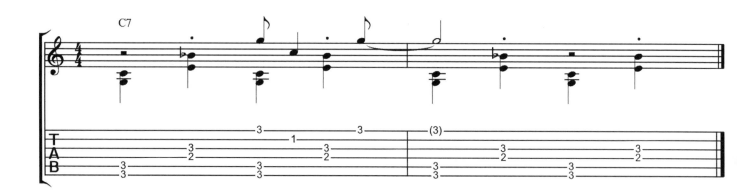

Now here's a full example of how Merle Travis might accompany his singing on this progression. Note the walking bass line that helps to connect the chords.

Example 6q:

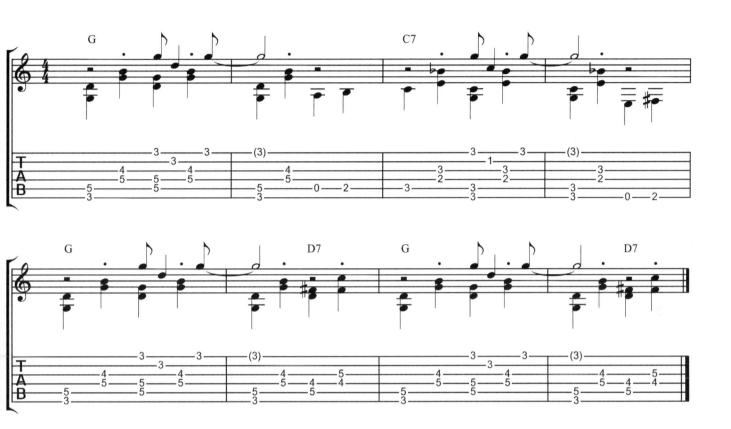

Here's an ending lick in the style of Merle. After playing the pattern on G from the last example, move up to the 7th fret and descend chromatically to the 5th.

Example 6r:

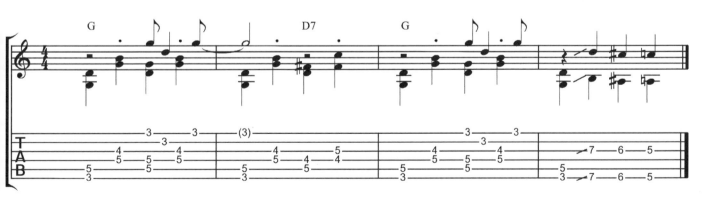

When studying Merle's style of Travis picking, it's important to remember that the melodies you play are dictated by which notes are available in the chord positions you choose. As you must always keep the thumb part steady, the melodies you play have to be available under the fingers.

Here are two simple melodies played on a barred G chord. To free the little finger to play melodies, the note normally fretted on the A string is omitted while a 6, 4, 6, 4 picking pattern is played with the thumb.

Example 6s:

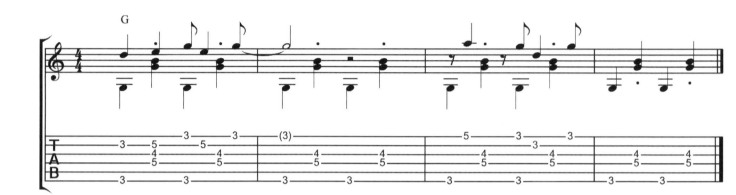

Here's the same example but with bars two to four shifted up the neck to outline a C major chord. Playing melodies through chord changes can often be this simple!

Example 6t:

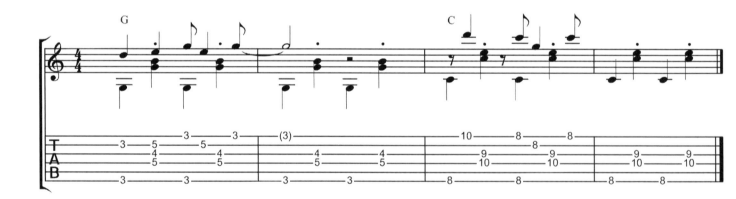

The following example develops the previous idea further by adding a walking bass line that connects the G major and C major chords. As you use the thumb to fret the bass note of each chord, it makes sense to also fret the walking bass line with the thumb too.

Example 6u:

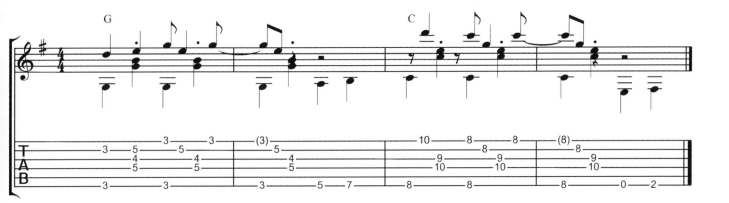

One useful way to add character to melodies found around chord forms is to bend notes, and the next example features bends on the B string. This technique is challenging as you need to bend just one just note while keeping the others in the chord static. Practice ideas like this slowly and remember to keep the definition between the muted thumb part and the ringing melody clear.

Example 6v:

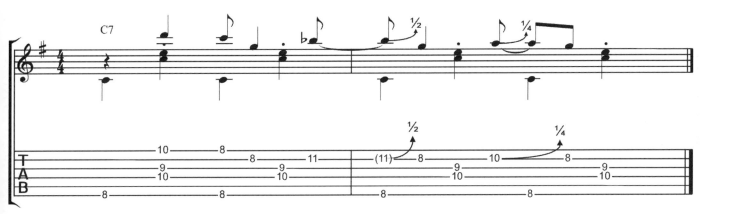

Here's a trickier example played on a turnaround. When tackling a complex example like this, learn the chord voicings first, as the melody consists of nothing more than available notes on the higher strings.

Example 6w:

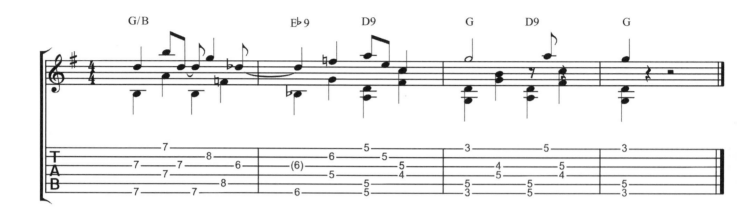

This next example draws from the classic fingerstyle tune, Cannonball Rag and moves around an E7, A7, D9, G major chord progression. The melody still fits around the chord voicings although the chromatic walk up on the D9 may require some isolated practice.

Example 6x:

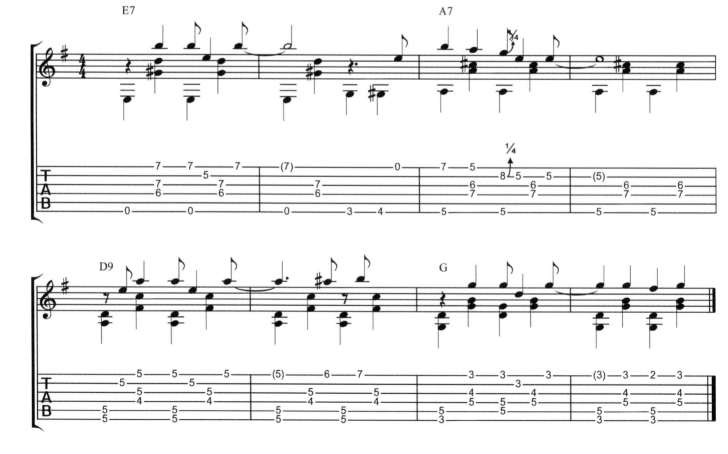

Here's an idea with a melody played in the bass. It begins on the D string to create something more melodic and moves down the E minor scale.

Example 6y:

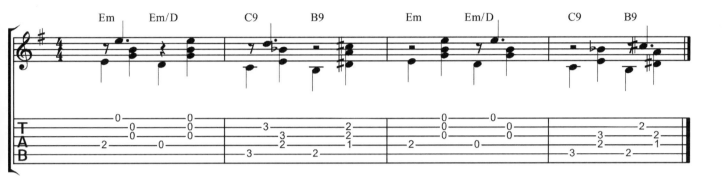

Aside from Travis picking, Merle's solos often featured an *ascending roll* pattern played with typically unique articulation. The thumb first plays two consecutive notes on adjacent strings before the index finger-picks a note on a third string.

Here's that technique applied to the top three notes of an E major chord and played with a triplet rhythm.

Example 6z:

That same idea can be played on any string grouping. Here it is applied to the D, G, and B strings.

Example 6z1:

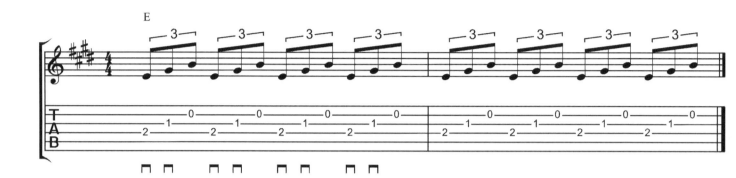

Now try alternating the index finger between the B and E strings.

Example 6z2:

Merle would often play this idea with an 1/8th note feel to create a two-bar phrase.

Example 6z3:

It's still possible to alternate the index finger note when playing this rhythm as this great little E7 lick shows.

Example 6z4:

Merle was extremely fond of this particular rhythm pattern and would often use it to outline chord progressions and add a little "flash" to his live performances. Here's one way he might outline the chords in Cannonball Rag.

Example 6z5:

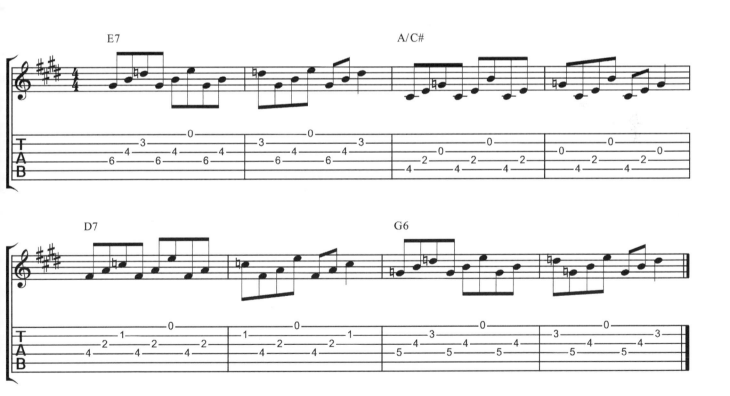

Here's one last way to outline the same chords. The next example is simply a case of picking a chord fragment and applying the "Merle roll" to proceedings!

Example 6z6:

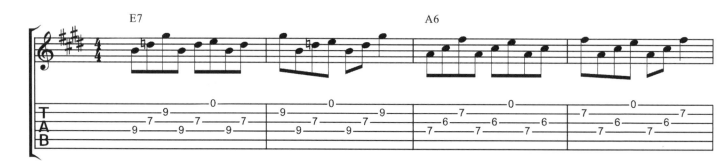

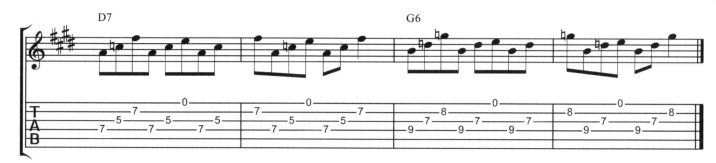

If you're struggling to play these rolls the way Merle played them, don't worry! The same is evidently true of many other great fingerstyle players who use other roll techniques discussed in later chapters.

These 1/8th note rolls were something that must have come quite naturally to Merle, and it's impossible to ignore that they have a unique sound compared to the more common multi-finger rolls we will study later.

Chapter Seven: Banjo Rolls

Before tackling the unique aspects of Chet Atkins' and Jerry Reed's playing, it makes sense to look at the development of Merle's banjo roll and develop some finger independence at the same time.

So far, you've only needed to use two digits on the picking hand; the thumb, and the index finger. The next step in developing more intricate ideas and increased speed is to introduce the middle finger.

The first concept to master is the art of the *forward roll*: Striking with the thumb pick, then the index finger, and finally the middle finger. This creates an ascending motion that feels like the hand is rolling forward.

Here's that technique applied to the top three notes of an E major chord.

Example 7a:

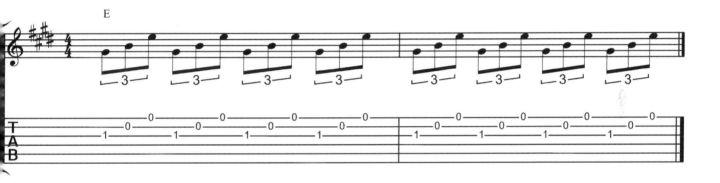

To develop the finger dexterity required to master the forward roll we will use a concept called "The Spanish Lap". This comes from a type of fitness training where you repeatedly jog the length of a sports pitch before sprinting the width. The idea is to ensure there's always gas left in the tank while increasing speed and stamina.

To apply this concept to the previous exercise, "jog" by playing play triplets on beats 1, 2, and 3, (three notes per beat) and then "sprint" by playing a sextuplet on beat 4 (six notes per click).

Example 7b:

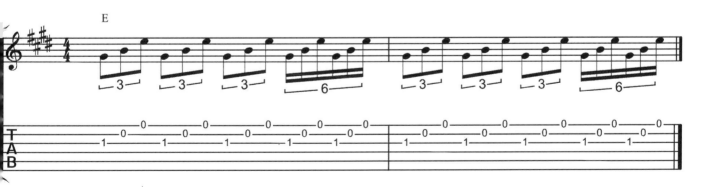

Here's the same idea but now jogging and sprinting for longer.

Example 7c:

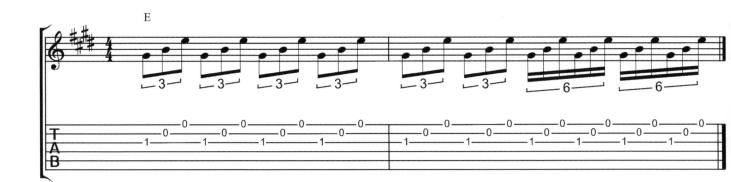

This concept can be applied to any string grouping and any set of notes, and will help you understand how it feels to play a forward roll.

Here's an example that combines open and fretted strings to create a repeating G note.

Example 7d:

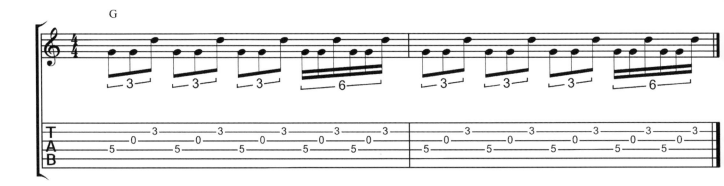

A problem I often see with my private students is what a classical teacher might describe as "lumpy" rhythms, meaning that the note divisions are not evenly spaced. Uneven rhythms often occur because it's easy to rush the roll and normally results in a longer amount of time between the notes played by the middle finger and thumb, than the ones played by the thumb and the index.

To even out lumpy rhythms, the best practice technique is to *offset* the start of the roll by a note. Here's a forward roll on a G major chord with the index finger placed on the beat instead of the thumb. This causes the roll to be displaced and is a great way to even out the rhythms between your fingers while developing great control in your playing.

Example 7e:

As you may expect, it's possible to displace the roll again in order to begin with the middle finger on the beat.

Example 7f:

Here's another take on the Spanish Lap concept that mixes 1/16th notes (four-notes-per-beat) and sextuplets (six-notes-per-beat).

Example 7g:

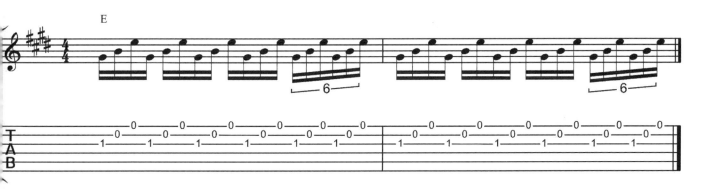

The next idea uses the same rhythm and moves between different string sets. Begin on the D, G, and B strings, before repeating the exercise on the G, B, and E strings.

Example 7h:

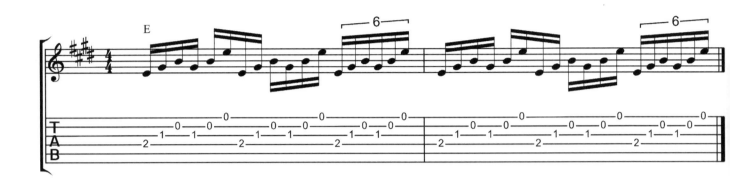

Here's the forward roll played on all six strings in groups of three.

Example 7i:

With the forward roll under your belt, it's time to turn your attention to the *backwards*, or *reverse roll*. As the name suggests, the reverse roll occurs when the roll moves from the middle finger to the thumb as demonstrated below.

Example 7j:

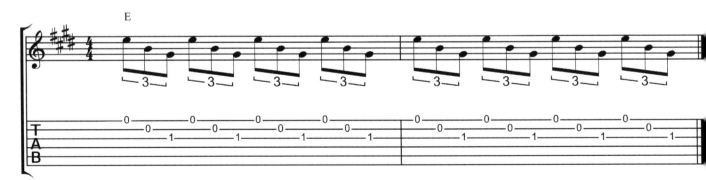

For most players, this picking mechanic feels more awkward than the forward roll and will normally require more practice. Weak spots in your technique often result in limitations to your music.

Here's the same reverse roll but now it's offset so the index finger falls on the beat.

Example 7k:

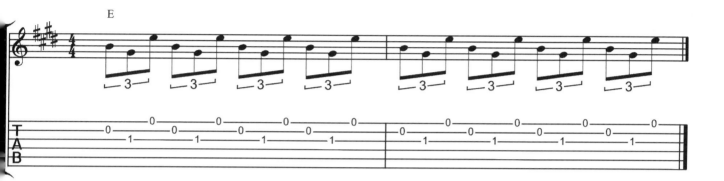

Here's a trickier example that sounds a lot more musical. From this point on, down-stroke (⊓) marks will be used in the notation to show the thumb picks.

Start with a thumb pick and then play a series of reverse rolls beginning on the middle finger.

Example 7l:

When speeding up rolls like this, the issue of tone arises. Many players decide to grow and maintain fingernails so the notes played with the fingers have a similar tonal attack to the notes played with the thumb pick. While there are more pros to this idea than cons, I always find comfort in the fact that Tommy Emmanuel plays with the flesh of his fingers. The best thing is to see what sound you prefer.

Here's another short lick that uses the reverse roll. Pay attention to the notes picked with the thumb and prepare to hit the reverse roll with the middle finger.

Example 7m:

Here's an idea often heard on banjo. The thumb plays the lowest note while the highest is plucked with the middle finger.

Example 7n:

This next example is a reverse roll variation of the previous idea. To spice things, up a grace note is added from Bb to B on the G string. The first note is played then immediately hammered to the second. Listen to the audio for reference.

Example 7o:

The following idea combines reverse rolls with the lick in example 7m to create something Jerry Reed might have played.

Example 7p:

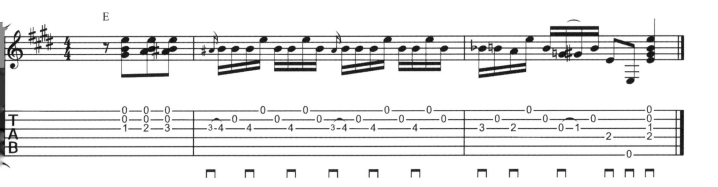

The next features a reverse roll and ringing open strings to mimic a classic banjo sound.

Example 7q:

The following idea is identical in the picking hand, but now the fretting hand outlines different chords to create something more musical.

Example 7r:

The following idea comes straight out of "The Danny Gatton Lick-Bag" and uses hammer-ons and forward rolls to unleash a flurry of notes.

Example 7s:

In this next example, the thumb alternates between the D and G strings while playing a reverse roll on the D, B and E strings. Start this one extremely slowly and gradually increase the speed over time until the picking mechanics feel as effortless as an alternating bass pattern.

Example 7t:

Here, the forward roll is applied across the stings in sets of three to create a ringing, scale-based idea.

Example 7u:

It's possible to get really "out there" with forward roll licks. The next idea is less about the scale used and more about just playing patterns.

Example 7v:

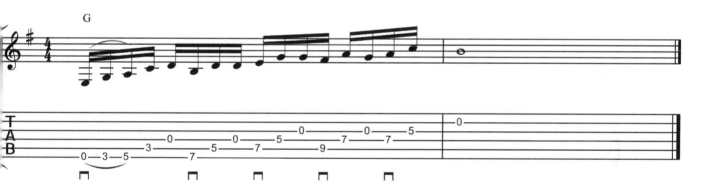

The example below relies on a strong reverse roll technique to build speed and was a favourite approach of Jerry Reed.

Example 7w:

The final example is a typical bluegrass-style lick that begins in the 5th-fret area and uses open strings to descend to an open G major chord.

Example 7x:

These are by no means an exhaustive list of banjo roll ideas (I'm sure they could fill a book by themselves!) but they're certainly enough to help you learn the vocabulary of the greats.

By now you should now have developed enough dexterity in your picking hand to tackle some of the techniques that distinguish Chet Atkins' playing from Merle Travis'. Let's take a look!

Chapter Eight: Chet Atkins Style

Chet Atkins was a master of the guitar who refined Merle's "trademark" Kentucky picking while bringing plenty of other innovative ideas to the country fingerpicking table.

The most obvious characteristic of Chet's playing was his cleaner and more refined thumb picking. Whereas Merle would play wide strokes with his thumb, Chet would stick closely to palm-muted single notes on beats 1 and 3 to imitate an upright bass, and use wider brushes with the thumb on beats 2 and 4 to give a little more harmony on the backbeat.

Here's an example of how Chet outlined a C major chord. His approach was incredibly deliberate and delicate when compared to Merles more rough and ready sound.

Example 8a:

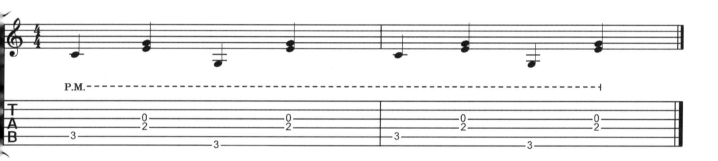

When adding a melody, those brush strokes on beats 2 and 4 really help to add a bigger sound to something that would otherwise be quite bare.

Example 8b:

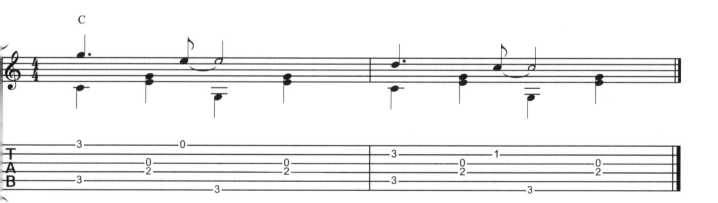

Here's a longer example with a melody that outlines an Amaj7 and E9 chord. Focus on those brush strokes with the thumb on 2 and 4 to get a bigger, more Chet-like sound.

Example 8c:

Go back through the whole book and play each example's bass part in the style of Chet Atkins. This is a great way to understand the difference between Chet and Merle's approaches to picking.

The other defining aspect of Chet's playing was his use of multiple picking-hand fingers to play more complicated melodies. The best way to get these ideas under your fingers is to practice them in isolation so they become effortless in real playing situations.

The first example uses the thumb on beat 1. The index finger the plucks the G string, before the middle and thumb pinch on beat 2.

Example 8d:

Here's an idea that feels a lot like a reverse roll. Remember; pay attention to the downward stems in the rhythm, these are the thumb strokes!

Example 8e:

This lick combines the previous two patterns into one longer example.

Example 8f:

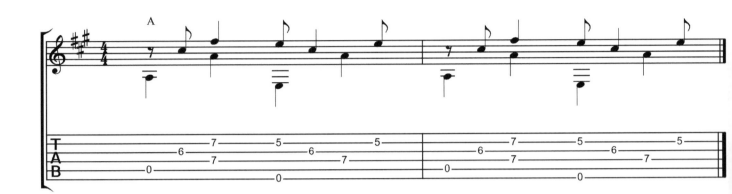

Here's a trickier idea based on a repeating reverse roll and creates a wonderfully syncopated sound.

Example 8g:

This next example takes influence from the Ragtime composer, Scott Joplin. Ideas like this often feel awkward as alternate notes are played by both fingers of the picking hand.

Example 8h:

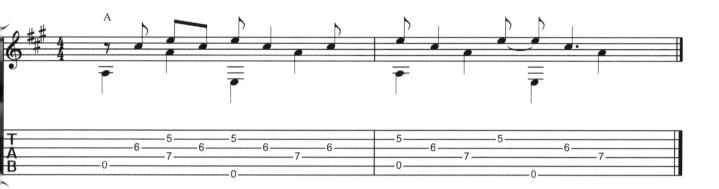

It's also possible to use both fingers on the picking hand to play double stops.

Example 8i:

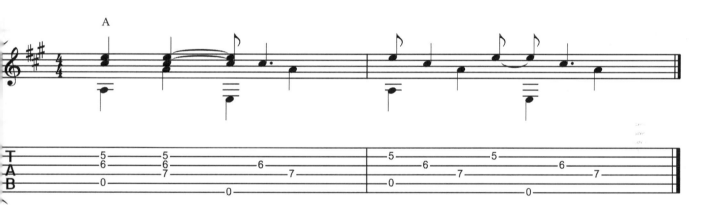

Here's a melodic fragment played on a 12-Bar Blues in E.

Example 8j:

t's possible to use any melodic pattern over a 12-Bar Blues. Here's an example that uses the same chords with a different melody.

Example 8k:

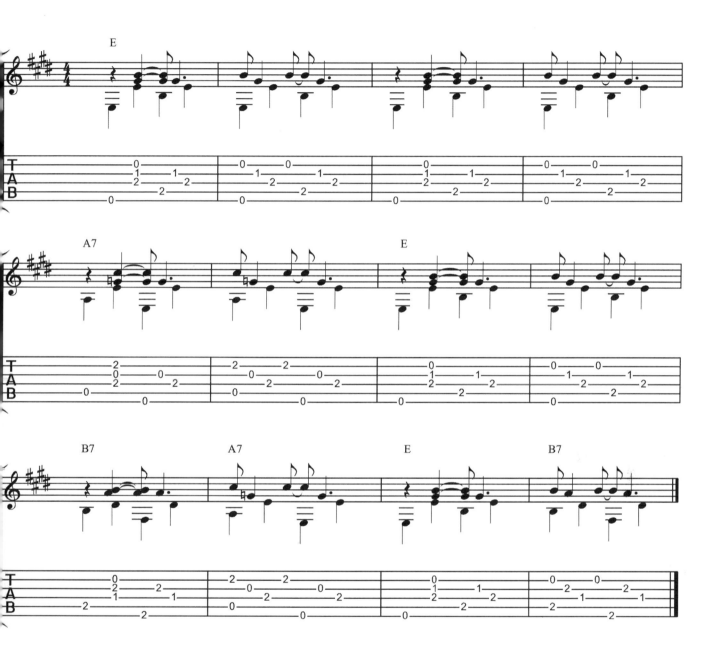

Here's a similar idea that uses some of the chord voicings from Chapter Five and creates a very different sound to playing open chords.

Example 8l:

This next example outlines an Am, C/G, D/F#, F major progression. Note the use of chord inversions to force a descending bass line of A, G, F#, F.

Example 8m:

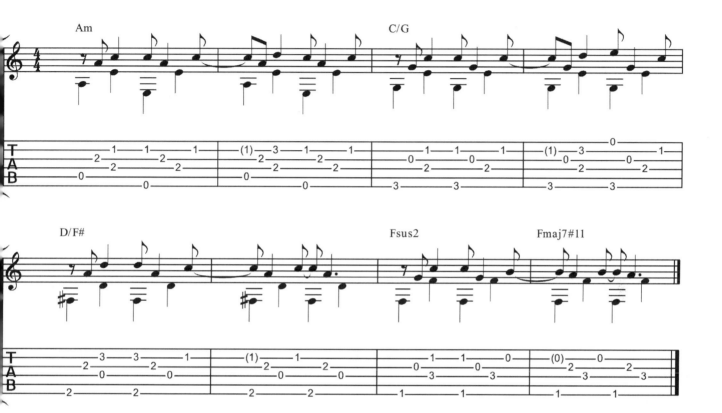

This idea is based on the the Lynyrd Skynyrd classic, Freebird. You'll quickly realize that it's easy to use these picking patterns on any chord progression to create an instant country-style makeover.

Example 8n:

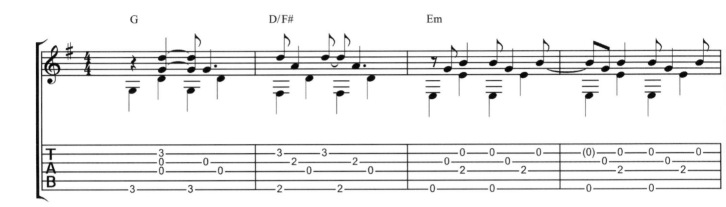

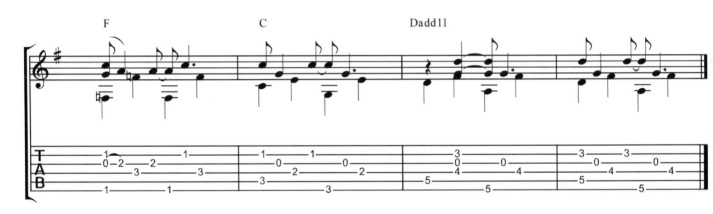

Here are some of the previous ideas applied to the melody of Freight Train. The reverse roll means you're able to play the melody while also filling in the melodic space with notes on the B string. It's important to make the melody notes nice and loud so they're not overpowered by the rhythm part.

Example 80:

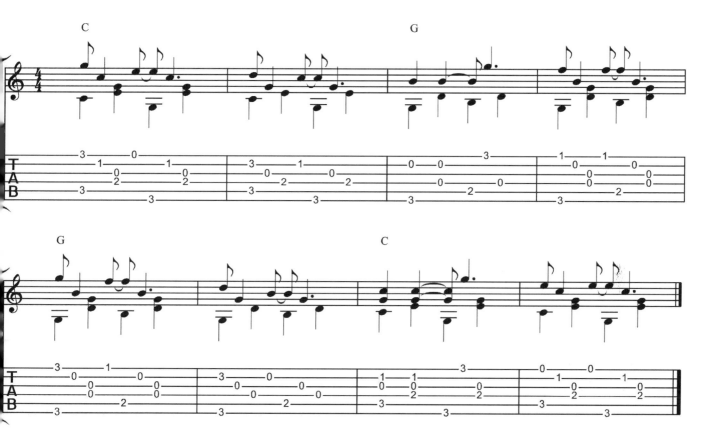

Here's a longer example that outlines the chords to the second section of Mr Sandman. There's no attempt to play the melody here; it's just a combination of the ideas presented in previous examples. The result sounds surprisingly full for something that's no more than standard chord grips.

Example 8p:

Harmonies

Another aspect of Chet Atkins' playing was to harmonise melodies with interesting note choices. For example, here's a simple melody on the B string.

Example 8q:

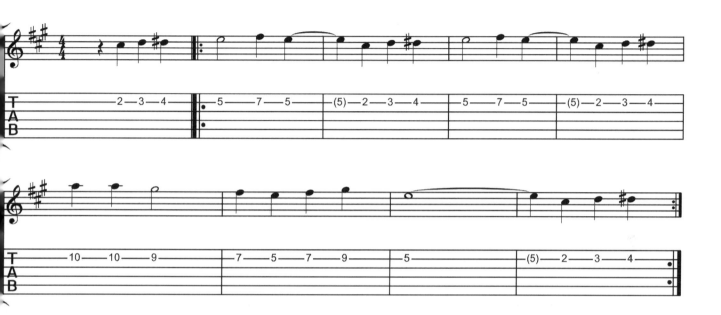

Now here it is again supported by notes played a 3rd lower on the G string.

Example 8r:

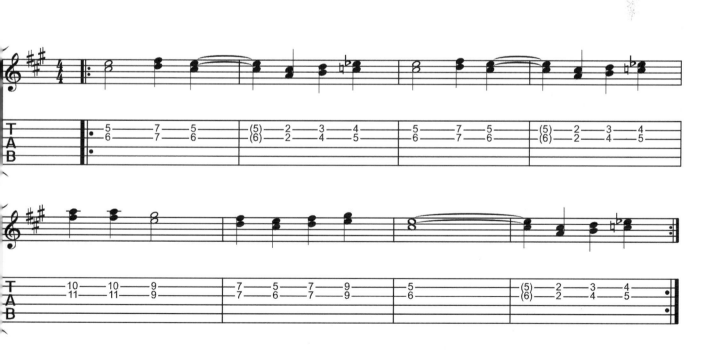

It's possible to use ideas like this with alternating bass patterns and you'll hear Chet it all the time. A great example is heard on his rendition of the Joplin classic, The Entertainer.

Example 8s:

Layering Parts

Chet was a master of layering parts. This was influenced by Les Paul, who created wonderfully intricate tracks with his wife Mary Ford through his pioneering work with multi-tracking.

Here's an example of how Chet Atkins might have used forward rolls to outline the chord changes to Cannonball Rag. Each chord voicing contains four notes and is executed with a three-string roll.

Example 8t:

To make things sound special on a record, Chet might track a harmony guitar to this guitar part. However, rather than being cold and clinical with precise theory, it can be rewarding to create a harmony part by simply using the same picking idea with different chord voicings.

Example 8u:

The example above could be played with a Merle-style roll technique, but Chet's multi-finger roll feels more natural to most players.

When played together, the two previous parts create a musical illusion that's impossible to play on one guitar but is incredibly dreamy. Ideas like these also work great in a live setting with two guitarists.

Harmonics

Another aspect of Chet's playing that helped to bring his arrangements to life was his use of harmonics.

Executing harmonics is simple; the finger is placed on the string directly over the indicated fret wire. The string is touched lightly, not pressed down, and then picked with the picking hand.

In the following example, the finger is placed over all six strings at the 12th fret and then strummed. The finger then moves to the 7th fret and finally the 5th. These are called natural harmonics.

Example 8v:

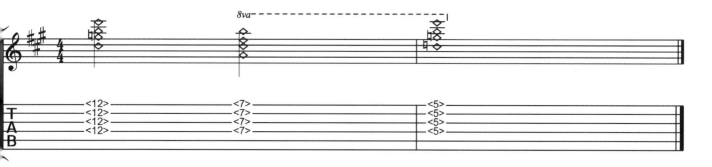

This next idea consists of single harmonics that ring into each other to create a beautiful wall of sound. Lift the fretting finger up as soon as each harmonic is played.

Example 8w:

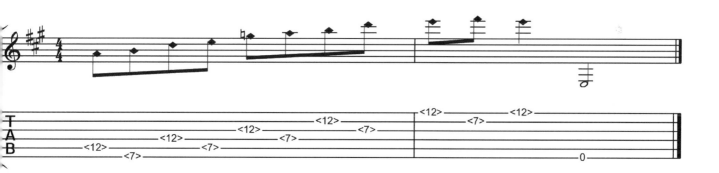

A development of natural harmonics is what's known as *artificial* harmonics. This technique requires you to fret a note and touch the string *12 frets higher* with the index finger of the picking hand. The string is then plucked with the picking hand thumb, resulting in a harmonic sounding one octave higher than the fretted note.

Here's that concept applied to an Amaj9 arpeggio.

Example 8x:

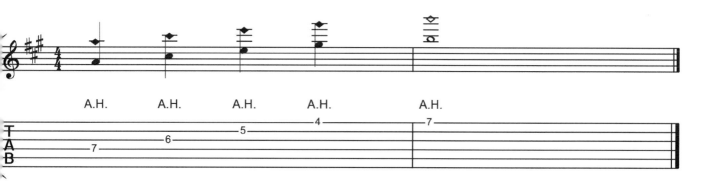

Chet Atkins often combine artificial harmonics with regular notes to create cascading runs that sounded like a harp. Chet credited Lenny Breau with the invention of this technique, though Lenny would often say he learnt it from Chet. Either way, it's a staple technique of fingerstyle guitarists.

In the following example, the chords are held down and allowed to ring. The D string is picked with the middle finger before an artificial harmonic is played on the E string with the thumb. The middle finger then reaches over to the G string while the harmonic moves to the A string, and so on.

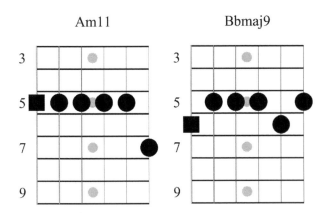

Example 8y:

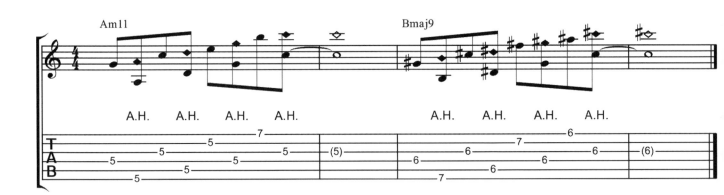

This final example expands on the previous idea by playing an artificial harmonic, then a pull-off two strings higher. This creates a regular descending scale idea with notes ringing into each other.

Example 8z:

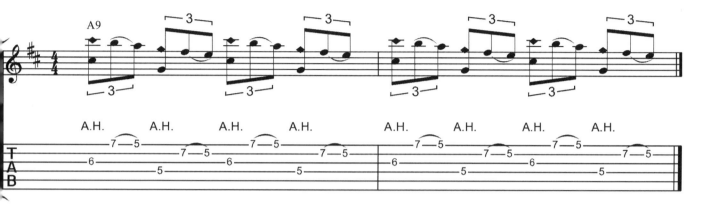

With 88 studio albums and numerous Grammy wins, Chet Atkins' repertoire was huge. His recorded material is a truly incredible collection and I encourage you to check out as much of it as possible. Many people end up devoting their entire lives to mastering the Chet Atkins sound.

There's a lot of magic, and plenty of influences to inspire your playing.

Chapter Nine: Jerry Reed Style

Often referred to as the "Alabama Wild Man", Jerry Reed Hubbard built an incredible career as a composer, singer, guitar player, television personality and actor.

Initially releasing numerous recordings for Capitol in the late '50s as a singer and becoming a sought-after session guitarist, most fans consider that his career truly begun in 1967 when RCA Victor released The Unbelievable Guitar and Voice of Jerry Reed.

Jerry recorded 33 albums for RCA Victor that showcased his phenomenal guitar playing, song writing (both for himself and artists like Elvis, and Tom Jones), and personality. Outside of his recordings, Jerry composed many guitar pieces recorded by others (Chet Atkins recorded many of them). In fact, Jerry never described himself as a guitar *player*, instead opting for the title "guitar thinker", as he would often conceive wonderful ideas and have someone else play them.

It's strange to note that while Jerry Reed is the natural evolution of Merle Travis and Chet Atkins, his playing is comparatively undocumented in guitar education. I'm inclined to believe it's due to the sheer difficulty of his playing and because it is so difficult to decipher. There are all manner of tricks and unorthodox techniques to learn to execute the ideas he dreamed up.

Jerry found his sound using nylon string guitars so the audio from this point will be recorded on my Godin Multiac. Nylon strings have a completely different sound to steel and feel easier to play, so why not give them a try?

To fully understand Jerry Reed's playing it's important to look at how his picking hand approach differed so greatly from Chet and Merle's. Jerry used a thumb-pick and three fingers, often tucking the index finger away and reserving it for alternate picking in tandem with the thumb pick.

The middle and ring fingers would often pair together when playing double stops and this is demonstrated in the following example on a C major chord. These double stops are plucked with the middle and ring fingers.

Example 9a:

The other thing to notice on the recording is that Jerry would often refrain from palm muting the bass part which resulted in a wild, untamed sound. This is a great texture to add to your arsenal of dynamic range.

The next stage when learning this style is to re-introduce the index finger and pluck additional notes *between* the notes played by the other fingers.

Here's the same example as before but now with the index finger added to the 'and' of beat 3.

Example 9b:

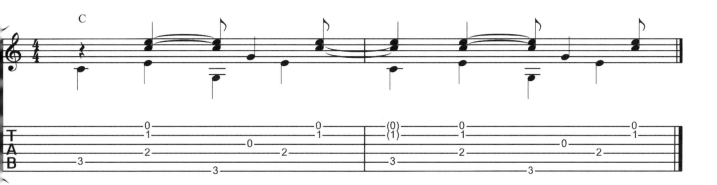

Revisit the early Chet Atkins fingerpicking examples in Chapter Eight, but now add in the 3rd finger. Here's an example based on a C major chord.

Example 9c:

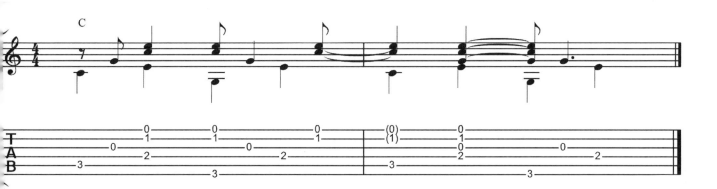

As with all the previously taught picking mechanics, we can apply these ideas on any chord progression to create a full-sounding piece of music.

This next example is a repeating mechanic applied on a C major to Am progression.

Example 9d:

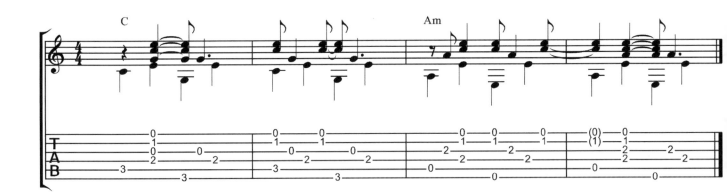

The following idea uses the same picking idea and applies it to chords higher up the neck.

Example 9e:

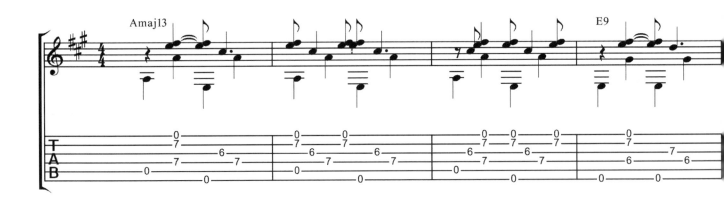

The Claw Pattern

So far, we have dealt with traditional backbeat grooves that accent beats 2 and 4, which is where you'd normally expect the snare drum to land. The backbeat has been the backbone of 90% of all rock and pop music for the last 80 years.

Jerry Reed often threw the traditional backbeat groove out the window and divided the bar into 1/8th note groupings of 3+3+2. The following example demonstrates this concept by showing the same phrase written in two different ways. The first bar is the rhythm written as you'd expect, while the second shows a grouping of 3+3+2.

Example 9f:

Jerry would play these ideas with constant 1/8th notes, and the bass note would fall in this 3+3+2 rhythm.

This idea is demonstrated on an A7 chord and should be picked as follows:

Group One: Thumb, index, middle-and-ring.

Group Two: Thumb, index, middle-and-ring.

Group Three: Thumb, middle-and-ring.

Example 9g:

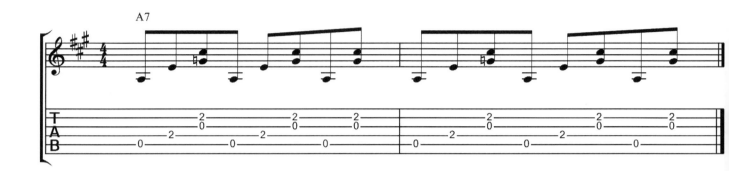

To bring ideas like this to life we can add a melody in the bass to move the chords forward.

This time I've added the ascending bass notes A, C#, E. To help you see this more clearly the bass line is written as a second voice with downward facing stems.

Example 9h:

Here's another pattern Jerry liked to play on an A7 chord. The bass part plays the notes A, E, G in the 3+3+2 groove.

Example 9i:

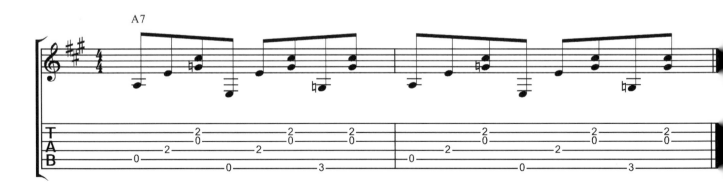

This next example is the same mechanic applied to an E7 chord.

Example 9j:

Here's a similar idea on an open D major chord. What you'll notice here is that the second finger needs to lift from the high E string and reach over to the A string to play the bass part.

Example 9k:

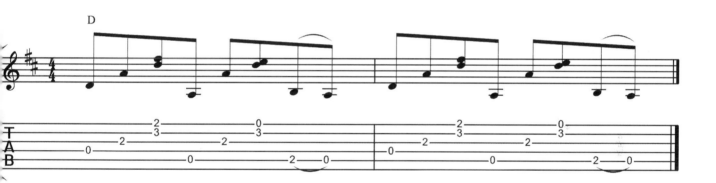

This feel is extremely common in Jerry Reed's music and is used in the songs, If I Promise, Long Gone, If it Comes to That, and The Claw, (these are just the ones on his first record!). These sorts of songs are so common that Reed fans refer to them all as "Claw tunes".

Here's a longer example inspired by Long Gone. It consists of nothing more than the chord ideas from the previous four examples.

Example 9l:

The following example draws influence from If I Promise, a tune made famous by Tom Jones. It shows that it's possible to change chords on any beat in the bar to make a riff.

Example 9m:

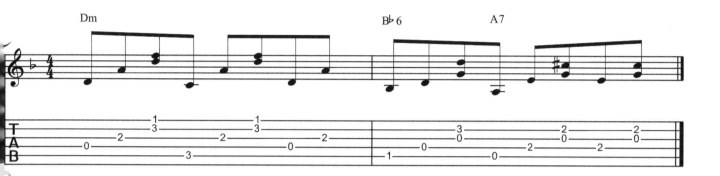

Here's an idea inspired by the Claw and mixes the claw pattern with melodic licks.

Example 9n:

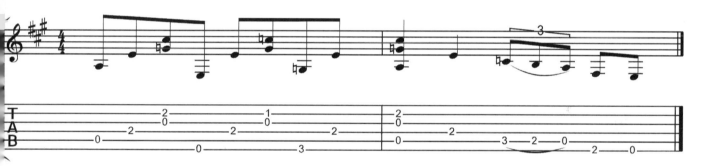

Altered Thumb-Picking

Alternate picking is easiest with a flat (normal) pick, as it's simple to adjust the amount of pick protruding from the fingers. It's almost impossible to make this adjustment with a thumb pick, therefore alternating between the thumb pick and a finger becomes the best option to play repeated notes on the same string.

Here is an example that features a simple alternating idea based around an A7 chord. The pick-strokes are indicated down and up as you'd expect. However, you should play all the upstrokes with the index finger.

Example 9o:

You may notice that this technique results in a choppier, staccato sound. This effect is a part of Reed's sound and a by-product of the technique: the index finger will mute the thumb-picked note as it's placed on the string to re-pick it.

Sometimes this picking technique results in playing phrases in a way that feels counter-intuitive. The next example features triple-stops on the middle strings that are played with the thumb, middle and ring fingers. These chords are then offset with an open A string picked with the index finger.

The feeling of playing the higher strings with the thumb and lower stings with the finger will feel awkward at first but stick with it: It's an essential technique used in many of Jerry Reed's tunes.

Example 9p:

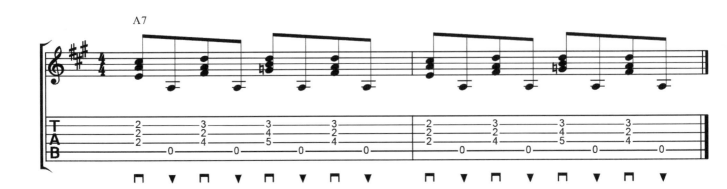

The technique is adapted to the music that needs to be played, not the other way around.

Example 9q:

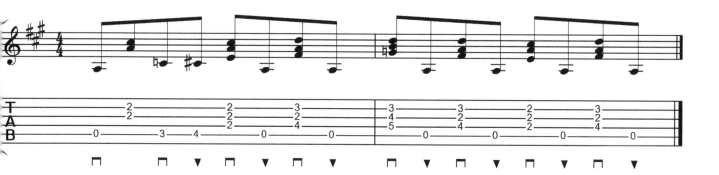

Counterpoint

Another trademark of Jerry's "guitar thinking" style is his use of two-part counterpoint.

Counterpoint is the name given to two parts moving independently of each other. A classical example of this would be the two-part harpsichord inventions of J.S. Bach where the left and right hands each play independent melodies that entwine with each other.

The easiest way to learn the counterpoint technique is by studying *contrary motion*: two lines moving in opposite directions.

Let's start with an ascending bass line, play this with the thumb pick only.

Example 9r:

Here's a melody that can be played with the index or middle finger.

Example 9s:

When played together with the pinch technique, the combination of these parts sounds completely different as the bass and melody lines both draw your attention.

Example 9t:

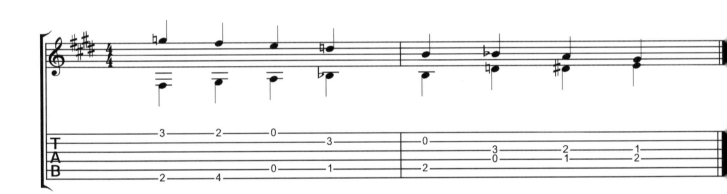

Here's an example that uses more variation to create more interest in the melody.

Example 9u:

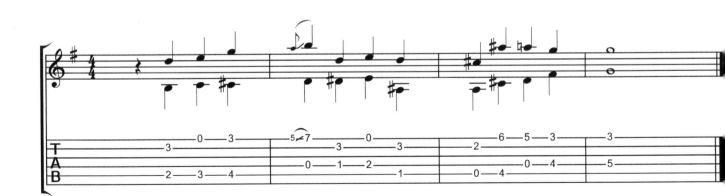

We can add syncopation to create a more engaging melody. In the following example, the top voice plays a melody over a supporting bass line for the first two bars before they switch roles in bars three and four.

Example 9v:

The next example is a little more taxing as it's played with an 1/8th note pulse and adds some pinched chords to the contrary motion.

Example 9w:

Now the bass part plays a steady descending line while the melody contains a variety of rhythms to create a delicately intricate phrase. These concepts can be tough to play cleanly and the trickiest part is allowing the bass notes to ring out against the melody, so keep those low notes held down!

Example 9x:

Jerry Reed's style was about being creative. It's almost impossible to improvise in this style (although Ted Greene seemed to manage it!), so don't beat yourself up if these examples don't fall under your fingers quickly. Reed imagined musical phrases and then worked out how to play them on the guitar afterwards. For you, this will begin as a slow process but before long you'll be able to mentally separate the bass and melody and it will quickly become easier to conceive these kinds of concepts.

Jerry's music is full of these mentally composed ideas so dig into some of his instrumentals to encourage your own imagination. A good place to start might be something like the classic track, Jiffy Jam.

Altered Tunings

The final aspect of Jerry Reed's style to consider was his willingness to experiment with the tuning of the guitar to make his ideas possible. The following examples all require some alteration to the guitar's tuning and sometimes also use a capo.

Dropped D tuning requires that you tune the 6th string down from the note E to a D. This is a quick and easy tuning to access; just play the E and D strings together and lower the pitch of the E until it matches that of the D.

Let's begin with a claw pattern on a D7 chord.

Example 9y:

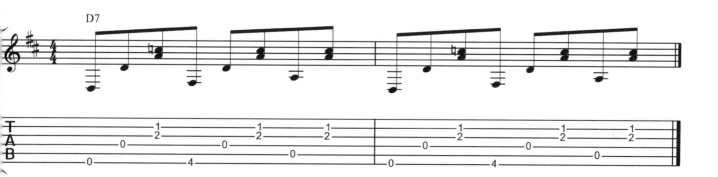

Here's an idea on a G7 chord. The G root note is no longer located at the 3rd fret as it's two frets higher. While this could be considered inconvenient, it has the benefit of allowing you to access a low D (the 5th of G) in the bass.

Example 9z:

When incorporated into a longer chord progression you get close to how Jerry played on songs like Wabash Cannonball.

Example 9z1:

It's possible to use altered tunings for some classical-inspired counterpoint ideas. This example features a cape on the second fret to keep the piece in E, but the smaller fret distances make fingering the notes on the E strin; (while baring) much easier.

Example 9z2:

A more unconventional tuning that Jerry Reed utilized (from low to high) was Db, Ab, Db, Gb, C, Eb. Thi is the whole guitar tuned down a semitone but with the low string dropped one further tone and the B strin; raised up a tone to C.

As complicated as it sounds, this tuning even made it on to some recording sessions with Elvis!

Here's a simple idea that introduces you to the above tuning. Use the thumb on the open 6th string and the middle and ring on the 2nd and 3rd strings. Keep the index finger free as Jerry would use it to build melodies on top of this basic idea.

Example 9z3:

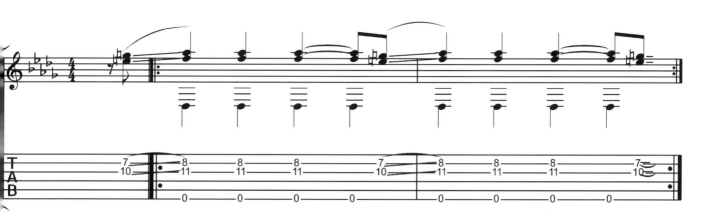

The index finger is now used to pick some syncopated melody notes on the D string.

Example 9z4:

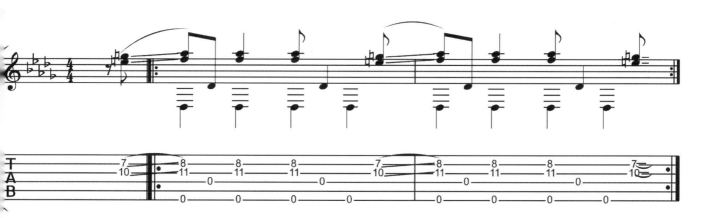

The following idea draws from the verse of Jerry's classic, Guitar Man. The thumb plays a simple ascending and descending pattern derived from the Db Mixolydian scale, while the middle and ring fingers play double stops on beats 2, 3, and the 'and' of 4.

Example 9z5:

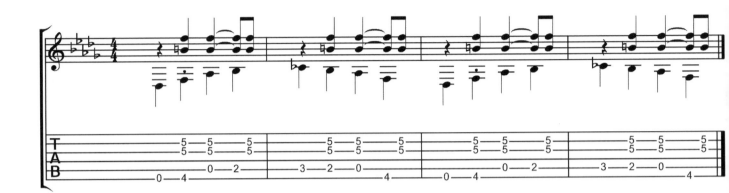

When the index finger is added, all these little syncopated "fill-in" notes take the riff to another level.

Example 9z6:

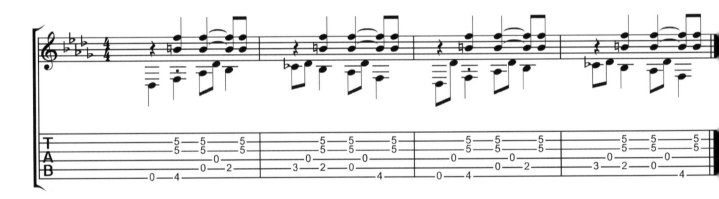

Here's a longer example that takes the previous picking pattern through a chord progression. The stretches required to keep this bass line going might seem a bit ridiculous, however the secret to playing them lies in the position of the guitar neck. Tilt it upwards so the headstock is level with your head.

Example 9z7

Another unique tuning Jerry used on songs like Tupelo Mississippi Flash and Alabama Wild Man was D, G, C, G, Bb, E. The lowest three strings are tuned down a tone and the 2nd string down a semitone to give a cool, open C9 tuning.

The following idea takes the technique in example 9o and develops it around this tuning. As before, use the pick directions to help distinguish between thumb strokes and upstrokes with the index finger.

Example 9z8

Here's a similar idea based around the 4th string (C). This would go perfectly with the previous example.

Example 9z9

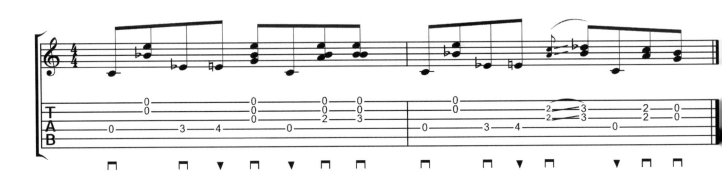

This final example takes the same picking idea but explores notes around the 6th string (D) to outline a new chord.

Example 9z10

The most important thing to do is to *listen*. Jerry has an array of blistering instrumentals, traditional country and light-hearted pop songs. The only way to appreciate him is to go and listen to as much as possible.

Chapter Ten: Are You from Wishy?

Now we've spent nine chapters deconstructing the fine art of country fingerstyle, we will combine all the concepts together into a more advanced solo piece sneakily titled Are You From Wishy? This is played in standard tuning.

For ease of study, I've presented the song in small sections so you can digest the parts slowly. The song can be played as one continuous piece and is available on the audio download.

The first section is a lead part in the style of Jerry Reed and features double stops and pull-offs.

Example 10a:

The first part of the tune outlines an A and D7 chord. These are played at the 5th fret to access the B melody note on the high E string.

Example 10b:

This section returns to the A7 chord, alternating between the open A root, an A played on the 7th fret D string with the 1st finger, and the open E string. The melody requires double stops, grace notes and open strings, so take it slowly.

Example 10c:

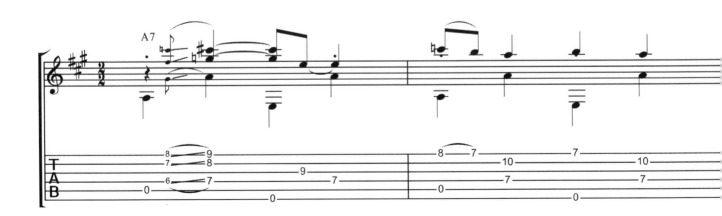

When returning to the A7 chord, a G note is held on the D string which allows the little finger to reach a C# melody note on the high E string.

Example 10d:

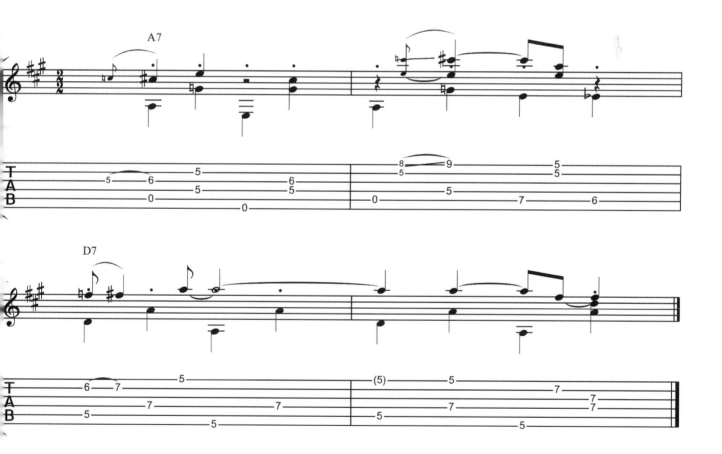

The next section moves to a B7 chord that precedes an E chord with an open E bass note. Notice how simple the melody is. It's simple in isolation but tricky when played together with the bass. Separate the parts by using palm mutes on the bass and let the melody ring out.

Example 10e:

When returning to the A7 chord, the melody is placed higher on the neck. The supporting bass part is one of the higher voicings covered in Chapter Five.

Example 10f:

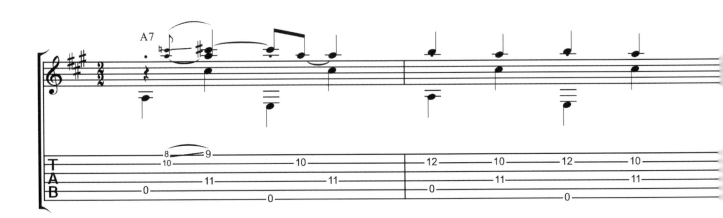

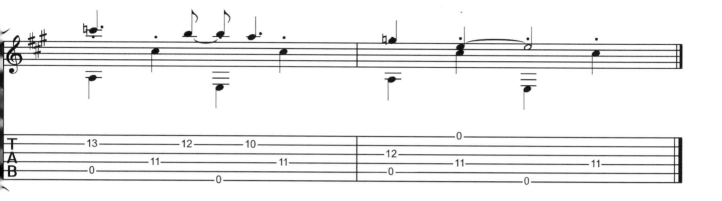

This lick moves up the neck to the 10th fret to outline a D7 chord. Many songs can be played by simply moving this single chord form up and down the neck.

Example 10g:

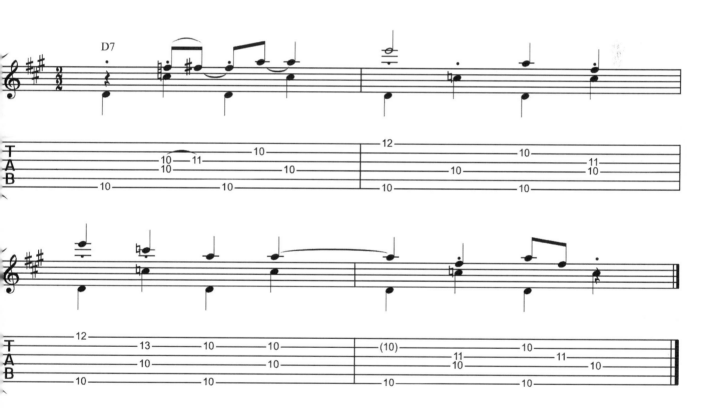

The next section outlines the A7 and D7 chords again but now with a different melody. On one hand, it's rewarding to know that so many different melodies can be found in each of these positions. On the other, it can be daunting to remember them all. Take each section slowly and appreciate the nuances in each one.

Example 10h:

The final section of this tune moves quickly from B7 to E7 before ending on A7. This is all played between the 5th and 9th frets using open strings in the bass to help outline the E and A7 chords.

Example 10i:

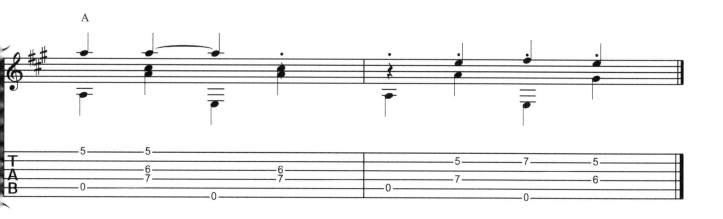

There's no hiding from the challenges in this chapter. While it's comparatively short, you may spend more time on these ideas than the ones earlier. Take as much time as you need to get each of these exercises down in detail before putting them together into one complete tune.

Conclusion

With these exercises under your belt you should be well on your way to playing competent country fingerstyle guitar. I'd like to offer you some thoughts to help you focus on the things that I feel matter most in your playing life.

It's not about speed, it's about moving people. Sometimes moving people will require playing quickly (perhaps to convey excitement), however, tone is always king. Listen to the notes you play and how each one sounds. Compare the projection heard from gypsy guitarists, vs picking lightly with the tip of the pick, imagine a melody being played with each, and when you might use one over the other

Timing is incredibly important. As well as playing along with the audio tracks, use a metronome and train your foot to tap along. The foot *taps* to the click, and you *play* to the foot. You aren't trying to train yourself to tap along to what you're playing; the pulse is the lifeblood of the music and your foot tells you where that is.

Here is a suggested listening list of my favourite country fingerstyle players. It's important to listen to country music as much as possible because you should understand the heritage that has been passed down from players to player, and eventually morphed into completely different genres.

- Buster B Jones – A Decade of Buster B. Jones
- Brent Mason – Hot Wired
- Chet Atkins – The Essential Chet Atkins
- Doyle Dykes – Virtuoso Fingerstyle Guitar
- Jerry Reed – The Unbelievable Guitar and Voice of Jerry Reed
- Marcel Dadi – La Guitare a Dadi
- Merle Travis – Sixteen Tons
- Scotty Anderson – Triple Stop
- Tommy Emmanuel – Endless Road
- Richard Smith – Slim Pickin'
- Martin Tallstrom – Acoustics
- Blind Blake – The Legendary Blind Blake

There are many players who use country techniques more sparingly and are just as important to study. Dig around to see who you can find, but do check out:

- Andy Mckee
- Brian Setzer
- Carl Verheyen
- Eric Roche
- Danny Gatton
- Joey Landreth
- Brad Paisley
- Johnny Hiland

Many lifetimes could be spent learning country fingerstyle guitar and I hope it excites you as much as it excites me. If you get half as much joy from playing it as I've had writing this book, then it's all been worth it.

Good luck!

Other Books from Fundamental Changes

The Complete Guide to Playing Blues Guitar Book One: Rhythm Guitar

The Complete Guide to Playing Blues Guitar Book Two: Melodic Phrasing

The Complete Guide to Playing Blues Guitar Book Three: Beyond Pentatonics

The Complete Guide to Playing Blues Guitar Compilation

The CAGED System and 100 Licks for Blues Guitar

Minor ii V Mastery for Jazz Guitar

Jazz Blues Soloing for Guitar

Guitar Scales in Context

Guitar Chords in Context

The First 100 Chords for Guitar

Jazz Guitar Chord Mastery

Complete Technique for Modern Guitar

Funk Guitar Mastery

The Complete Technique, Theory & Scales Compilation for Guitar

Sight Reading Mastery for Guitar

Rock Guitar Un-CAGED

The Practical Guide to Modern Music Theory for Guitarists

Beginner's Guitar Lessons: The Essential Guide

Chord Tone Soloing for Jazz Guitar

Chord Tone Soloing for Bass Guitar

Voice Leading Jazz Guitar

Guitar Fretboard Fluency

The Circle of Fifths for Guitarists

First Chord Progressions for Guitar

The First 100 Jazz Chords for Guitar

100 Country Licks for Guitar

Pop & Rock Ukulele Strumming

Walking Bass for Jazz and Blues

Guitar Finger Gym

The Melodic Minor Cookbook

The Chicago Blues Guitar Method

Heavy Metal Rhythm Guitar

Heavy Metal Lead Guitar

Progressive Metal Guitar

Heavy Metal Guitar Bible

Exotic Pentatonic Soloing for Guitar

The Complete Jazz Guitar Soloing Compilation

The Jazz Guitar Chords Compilation

Fingerstyle Blues Guitar

The Complete DADGAD Guitar Method

Country Guitar for Beginners

Beginner Lead Guitar Method

The Country Fingerstyle Guitar Method

Beyond Rhythm Guitar

Rock Rhythm Guitar Playing

Fundamental Changes in Jazz Guitar

Neo-Classical Speed Strategies for Guitar

100 Classic Rock Licks for Guitar

The Beginner's Guitar Method Compilation

100 Classic Blues Licks for Guitar

The Country Guitar Method Compilation

Country Guitar Soloing Techniques

Printed in Great Britain
by Amazon